PROBLEMS AND SOLUTIONS IN URBAN SCHOOLS

Front Cover: Original Artwork by Bob Smith.
Blacksmiths Cards & Prints, Altadena, California

PROBLEMS AND SOLUTIONS IN URBAN SCHOOLS

Edited by
Gwendolyn M. Duhon

Mellen Studies in Education
Volume 57

The Edwin Mellen Press
Lewiston•Queenston•Lampeter

Library of Congress Cataloging-in-Publication Data

Problems and solutions in urban schools / [edited by] Gwendolyn M. Duhon.
     p. cm. -- (Mellen studies in education ; v. 57)
    Includes bibliographical references.
    ISBN 0-7734-7542-7
    1. Urban schools--United States. 2. School improvement programs--United States. I.
Duhon, Gwendoyn M. II. Series.

    LC5131 .P74 2001
    371'.009173'2--dc21

                      00-050025

This is volume 57 in the continuing series
Mellen Studies in Education
Volume 57 ISBN 0-7734-7542-7
MSE Series ISBN 0-88946-935-0

A CIP catalog record for this book is available from the British Library.

Copyright © 2001 The Edwin Mellen Press

The Edwin Mellen Press
Box 450
Lewiston, New York
USA 14092-0450

The Edwin Mellen Press
Box 67
Queenston, Ontario
CANADA L0S 1L0

The Edwin Mellen Press, Ltd.
Lampeter, Ceredigion, Wales
UNITED KINGDOM SA48 8LT

Printed in the United States of America

Table of Contents

3

Foreword

Current societal perception is that urban education in America is under attack. These perceptions, which permeate all segments of society, impact the thinking and attitudes of Americans about the purpose of educational institutions and the academic success of students. These perceptions serve as the basis for criticisms of urban schools. A realization is surfacing that America needs to enter the new millennium poised to address the educational issues affecting the academic success of urban students. This book contains the work of professionals across several different academic disciplines offering solutions through various teaching strategies, theoretical approaches, and leadership models. The major purpose of this book is to create a level of consciousness that will motivate everyone in society to make a commitment to improving the quality of education in American's urban schools.

Rose Duhon-Sells, Ph.D.
Senior Vice-President of Academic Affairs,
The Union Institute
Cincinnati, OH

Preface

America's urban public schools have a formidable task: to
meet the academic, emotional, social, and developmental needs of
a variety of students from a myriad of cultures and backgrounds.
Few urban public schools are prepared to meet this challenge-due
to limited budgets, over-worked teachers, and apathetic
communities. Teacher preparation programs also face a difficult
challenge in adequately training teachers to be effective in urban
settings. This book, *Problems and Solutions in Urban Schools*,
attempts to address these challenges by providing new insights to
existing concerns. It contains the work of professionals across
several different academic disciplines offering solutions through
various teaching strategies, theoretical approaches, and leadership
models. The authors recognize the issues faced by urban schools
and offer common sense approaches that can improve the quality
of education in America's urban schools settings. They strategize
ways parents, educators, and others concerned with the welfare of
children and youth in urban schools to overcome the negative
attitudes and actions that plague urban schools. The reader will be

5

able to obtain ideas from the authors for creating learning environments that meet the many academic needs of urban students.

This book contributes a body of knowledge based on current research, which will be beneficial to parents, professionals across academic disciplines, and others who are concerned, committed to, and compassionate about promoting change in American urban schools and society. The major purpose of this book is to create a level of consciousness that will motivate everyone in society to make a commitment to improving the quality of education provided in today's urban school settings.

Gwendolyn M. Duhon
Editor

CHAPTER 1

An Urban School Dilemma—The At-Risk Student

Tony J. Manson, Ph. D., Assistant Professor
Middle Tennessee State University
Murfreesboro, Tennessee

Joseph Jefferson, Ph. D.,
Professor, Chair of Counseling and Leadership
Texas Southern University
Houston, Texas

Introduction

This chapter is a history of the treatment and consideration given in American education to students who are now classified as "at-risk" In our urban schools. The term is a relatively recent coinage, reflecting the newness of educators' recognition that a measurable portion of students, beyond those with evident physical or mental handicaps, have special educational needs. Comprehending what educators mean by the term "at-risk," which has become more an acknowledgement of economic disadvantage and less a categorization of biological abnormalities is essential to understanding the ways in which such children have been treated throughout the development of the educational system in the United States.

Concepts and Semantics

Historically, the concept of compulsory education for all as an individual right and a societal necessity developed while the United States grew and matured into an industrialized nation. The changing way in which educators have looked on the problems presented by "at-risk" children represents a striking model for their refinement in thinking about education as a whole. From early colonial times, when schooling was considered to be primarily the responsibility of the family, to the modem age of widespread societal involvement in educational systems that attempt to include the entire young population, the varying needs of the individual child continue to pose a complicated challenge to each successive generation.

Educators began to talk about "at-risk" students during the 1970s but still have not agreed on a precise definition of the tern. While it may include students with physical or emotional handicaps, learning disabilities, or other special education needs, "at-risk" has come to focus primarily on children of poverty, those

8

from poorer single-parent homes, and those without homes at all. Stephen B. McCamey (1991) writes:

> "At-Risk" means different things to different people. To the teacher, "At-Risk" may mean the student is "At-risk" for failure, which will result in retention at the end of the year. To the social worker, "At-Risk" may mean that an abused child is "At-Risk for becoming an abusive parent. To the social or economic analyst, an "At-Risk" child is one who is born out of wedlock, grows up in poverty and is likely to repeat the cycle (p. 3).

Barbara Z. Presseisen (1991) writes, " 'At-risk' appears to be the latest semantic label of American education attached to several groups of students who have experienced difficulty or, in fact, failure in their careers as learners" (p. 5). She lists some of the other labels that "at-risk" has come to encompass: "culturally deprived, low income, dropout, alienated, marginal, disenfranchised, impoverished, underprivileged, disadvantaged, learning disabled, low performing, low achieving, remedial, urban, ghetto, language-impaired" (p. 5). The term most often links children whose learning difficulties arise from the complications of poor economic backgrounds.

A Symptom (Dyslexia)

Dyslexia is among the most common learning disabilities exhibited by at-risk children; it is a disability that has only recently been widely examined and analyzed. While a diagnosis of dyslexia does not automatically place a child at risk, this barrier to learning is often present in those children facing other obstacles, adding to their difficulties in the classroom. Presseisen (1991) contends, "As much as 15 percent of the entire population may exhibit symptoms of various handicapping conditions akin to dyslexia" (p. 9). The "at-risk category also includes those whose cannot speak or read English well, since this places students at a distinct disadvantage in the classroom, where most progress is tied to reading, listening, and speaking proficiency.

The State of Education

Lawrence A. Cremin (1976) notes that public education arose out of "the interest of equalizing opportunity and encouraging individual development and at the same time achieving a certain measure of socialization for public ends" (p. 124). As cities and factories grew, American society realized the unusefulness of being able to communicate with thousands of fellow citizens able to read street signs, calculate transactions, and record sales orders. Perhaps even more important, society began to see the value of schools in providing a sense of community, which was no longer possible to achieve in any other way within the swelling urban environment.

10

The rise of cities and the new middle class made at least minimal education for the poor a social imperative; despite their best efforts, members of the upper class were unable to completely avoid contact with the lower classes in the modern world. The United States has grown to the point that the handicapped, the very slow, the very young, the emotionally disturbed, the gifted have all received attention to form the concept of inclusion. Also, the concept that education should be available and mandatory for all children has led to the belief that tax-supported schools are necessary to a democratic society, an idea that was not universally accepted at first. In the early part of this century, at-risk students were most often defined by their economic disadvantages, this disparity often resulted in an even greater educational imbalance in high-density urban centers, a situation not foreseen by scholars and educators who championed universal education as a democratic ideal.

Atkinson and Maleska (1962) write, "Several million American children are handicapped in ways that demand specialized education facilities. A report made to the Fourth White House Conference in the 1940s, reported that approximately 30 percent of all children in American schools could be grouped into what its writers termed at the time the "delicate child" class. In the

11

1990s that figure has at least tripled. As educators started to address the particular educational needs of "delicate" children openly, they developed separate classes and in many cases separate schools within the same district to deal with these children. Separating out students, however, proved to be a less-than-popular concept, and the arguments gave way to "mainstreaming" special needs student back into regular classrooms as much as possible. Today these facilities are no different than any other facility on a high school campus. In many cases they are no more than a room or a section of the school that is usually forbidden for 'regular students' to be near. In fact many school district have what is known as 'Alternative Schools'. These schools are designed specially for students at-risk of dropping out of school because of most anything (addictions, attendance, attitude, behavior, etc.).

Categories

The "at-risk" diagnosis is a recent attempt by educators to gather together all those categories of children with problems that prevent them from progressing unaided within a regular classroom. These include students with attention deficit disorders (ADD), as well as those deemed educable mentally impaired (EMI), educable mentally retarded (EMR), emotionally impaired (EI), and even

12

those informally diagnosed as "troublemakers". Valerie Polakow (1993) quotes a Phi Delta Kappa study in which "the authors begin with the assumption 'that children are at risk if they are likely to fail - either in school or in life' " (p. 153).

However, one of the older labels, learning disabled (LD), continues to provide a subtly different meaning in the educational debate. Gerald Coles (1987) explains:

> The category was introduced in the U. S. schools in the 1960s as one of the means of explaining a handicapping condition which many professionals and middle-class parents considered unaddressed by existing educational classifications... [They] thought that special-education classifications such as "mentally retarded' or emotionally disturbed" and prevailing social-science categories for explaining academic failure such as "culturally deprived" seemed more appropriate for children from minority and poor communities, not children from the middle class (p. xiii).

Coles observed that in recent years educators have applied the LD diagnosis much more broadly, prompting middle-class parents to seek other labels in order to maintain distinctions between students who enjoy economic advantage and children of poverty. "At-risk" has become one of the most useful of these labels.

Otherness

Increasingly, however, this kind of political use of educational diagnoses has come under fire. Polakow (1993) contends, "We call [students] 'at risk' less out of outrage and compassion than because their condition threatens our security and comfort, our children, our schools, our neighborhoods, our property values. Their otherness places us 'at-risk' " (p. 43). Coles (1987) summarizes a number of studies showing that minority children tend to be represented in "at-risk" grouping in disproportionately high numbers in many parts of the country, suggesting that such categories "allowed discrimination to continue but in a less blatant form" (p. 206).

As America began to accept their need for universal free education, educators only belatedly came to see that this would require systems flexible enough to accommodate individual differences. They grouped these differences into diagnosable categories, naming and renaming categories for semantic clarity and political fashion. "At-risk" is the most recent category name to specify a group of students always present in the population, the "deserving poor, " children who have never fit easily into any mainstream conception of American education.

14

Bibliography

Atkinson, C., & Maleska, E. T. (1962). The Story of Education. Philadelphia: Chilton.

Duhon, G., and Manson, T. J. (2000). Preparation, Collaboration and Emphasis on The Family in School Counseling For The New Millennium. Lewiston, New York: The Edwin Mellen Publishing,

Coles, G. (1987). The Learning Mystique: A Critical Look at "Learning Disabilities". New York: Pantheon.

Cremin, L. A. (1976). Traditions of American Education. New York: Basic.

McCarney, S. B. (1991). The At-Risk Student in Our Schools: A Model intervention Program for the At-Risk Student's Most Common Learning and Behavioral Problems. Columbia, MO: Hawthorne Educational Services.

Polakow, V. (1993). Lives on the Edge: Single Mothers and Their Children in the Other America. Chicago: University of Chicago.

Presseisen, B. Z. (1991). At-Risk Students: Defining a Population. In K.M. Kershner & J. A. Connolly (Eds.), At-Risk Students and School Restructuring (pp. 5-11). Philadelphia: Research for Better Schools.

CHAPTER 2

Is Instruction Equal for Everyone?
A Look at Gender Equity

Tony James Manson, Ph.D.
Middle Tennessee State University
Murfreesboro, Tennessee

Bonita Jones Manson, Ph. D.
Middle Tennessee State University
Murfreesboro, Tennessee

Karen Martin, Ph. D.
Southern University at New Orleans
New Orleans, Louisiana

Is Instruction Equal for Everyone?

<u>A Look at Gender Equity</u>

Gender equity has become a priority in the school curriculum. One reason is that women have been asked to learn the experience of men and accept them as representative of all human experiences. When they are unable to do this (match this masculine knowledge to their own lives), the women- not the facts, theories, and curricula have been termed deficient (Kohlberg, 1981; Vaillant, 1977). The challenge is to change the schools and

17

curricula to reflect the perspectives of all students. This step may help to eliminate bias that might occur when the masculine experience is the standard. In the past, women used legislation to help prioritize change. Title IX of the Educational Amendment Act of 1972, the Women's Educational Equity Act in 1975, and the Vocational Amendment Act of 1976 as well as other legislation from 31 states prohibited sex discrimination in primary and secondary school programs receiving federal funds. The legislation precipitated some changes, but researchers such as Myra Sadker (1989), surveyed practitioners who viewed the educational movement as doing very little to promote educational equity or even close the gender achievement gap.

Today, we must teach equity in the classroom. Without equity in schools, students will not experience true educational excellence. The goals of gender equity are:

> -to protect students' rights to an equal education free of discrimination on the basis of sex, marital and/or parental status;
> -to help students free themselves from limiting, rigid sex-role stereotypes and sex bias;
> -to assist students to explore and participate in a broader range of educational programs and activities leading to higher paying and/or more satisfying careers;
> -to help students understand, think about, and prepare for a future characterized by change, especially in male and female roles, relationships, and in careers.

-to evaluate students about personal and social economic changes, by traditional socialization of maLe and females, or which affect girls and women dispartionately (Rodenstein, 1990).

The educators' goal is to make sure that all students have a fair chance to learn and develop as individuals. Any practice that discriminates or reinforces competitive individualism must be changed. The female omission from the textbook sends the wrong messages to females. This message is intensified when the teachers do not point out or confront the omission. Furthermore, when teachers add their stereotypes to the curriculum bias in books, the message becomes even more damaging. Our daughters learn that to be female is to be the absent partner in the development of our nation (Sadker, 1994). An interesting study was conducted in Michigan, with a little under 2,000 students, about what it was like to be male or female at school. The students interviewed felt that girls were treated differently in schools and by high school, this number had risen to 76 percent. The question becomes, what can we do to provide equitable education to all students so that they will have a positive experience in school?

The school curriculum can be changed to reflect the needs of all students. It is no longer okay to limit the expectations about abilities, interest, skills and temperament by gender. We can no

19

longer say gender roles are biologically inherited; there is no scientific proof (Klein, 1985). Gender biased thinking that has resulted in the lack of awareness and expectations for women must be counteracted. The goal is for all persons to be independent rather than dependent in their daily lives and to be truly financially self-sufficient. Creating better options, skills, and expectations opens doors to newer opportunities. Education provides options. The more a person has, the better the options and opportunities become.

Girls start out ahead of boys in speaking, reading and counting. Their academic performance is equal to that of boys in math and science in the early grades. However, as girls progress in school, their achievement in these subjects significantly declines (Sadker, Sadker, & Long; 1993). In fact, many girls do not even take courses in math when they reach high school. The gender gap in mathematics performance and attitudes was attributed by several authors to course enrollment in high school (Lindbeck and Dambrot, 1986). Many areas in college require a math background. Thus, when females lack mathematical background, they limit their opportunities to participate in areas requiring math in college and later in the job market. A question asked in recent research was, "Why are women less interested in taking mathematics courses, especially at an advanced level?" Several researchers (Betz, 1978; Fennema and Sherman, 1977; Gressard and Loyd, 1987; Lindbeck and Dambrot, 1986) have all suggested that math anxiety is an inhibiting factor in both the participation in and learning of mathematics. Fennema (1980) suggested that this anxiety level along with low self-confidence in math courses are important factors that explains the sex-related differences.

Women have also been deterred from math because it has been stereotyped as a "masculine subject" (Shashaani, 1995). It is this stereotypic view about math and science that parents and teachers support (Shashaani, 1993; Jacobs, 1991). Further research by Sells (1990) found a strong relationship between taking advanced mathematics in high school and the support and encouragement shown by parents, teachers, and peers. A model by Eccles and his colleagues (1983) was developed to determine academic achievement behavior. According to this model, students' career choices are influenced by (1) socio-cultural environment including socialization forces, gender-role beliefs, and cultural norms; and (2) psychological factors such as expectations for success, short and long range goals, subjective task value, and perceptions of task difficulty (Shashaani, 1995). Sometimes

21

females are very successful in math and science courses but they are not provided the same feedback that the males receive. Sadker (1994) reported a male teacher's response to the male students in his physics class who had scored less than the three female students on an exam: "Boys, you are failing. These three pretty cookies are out scoring you guys on every test!" (Sadker, 1994). Not only did the teacher not compliment the girls, he did not even address them as females or by their name. Both teachers and parents are influential in encouraging students to take more math or science courses. If encouragement is not given, students tend to not further their studies in this area.

Parents seem to have lower levels of educational expectations for their daughters, especially in the areas of mathematics and science (McCoby and Jackin, 1973; Eccles et al., 1983). Yee and Eccles (1988) reported that parents attributed their daughters' math success to effort and their sons' math success to talent. Parents are children's first teachers and their roles are very powerful. It is important that they send out positive messages to their children. Children do not need to feel that they are different just because of their gender. Gender bias such as this discourages girls even though their grades are as high as boys on math tests. Many myths exist between males and females as to which group

22

actually gains the favor of the academic world. What educators need to do is to examine the areas of specialization that males are in as opposed to those of their female counterparts. Teachers and counselors often advise stereotypical careers to their students. This behavior may result in less potential for females, while offering greater potential for males. The goal is to eliminate roadblocks by providing equity for all students. If females choose not to study math or science, they are filtered out of careers that remain overwhelming and solidly male.

The career connection is also made through sports in high school. Athletics is important in shaping the lives of the male students by providing opportunities for them to demonstrate leadership, self-confidence and courage. Sports is seen as a vehicle for shaping boys into men who will lead society. This same concept should apply to girls. However, girls have been historically barred from sports until recently. Their only experience in sports was in segregated classes with poor equipment and fewer resources. After the passage of Title IX in 1972, female participation in interscholastic sports programs has increased but it still lags behind boys' participation.

Teachers need to expand the examples used in the classroom and go beyond the traditional world of males in their

23

discussion. This sometimes can be difficult because attitudes are hard to change. James Banks (1989) introduced a six-part curriculum of articles that provided future and experienced teachers with knowledge, insight, and understanding needed to work effectively with both male and female students with exceptional abilities who come from various social classes, ethnic, religious, and culture groups. James Banks says, "A major assumption is that substantial reforms must be made in schools to give each student an equal chance to succeed academically" (1989). Teachers also need to provide young women with a curriculum that values them and teaches them about their contributions in history. Through learning, all students can draw on the full range of life experiences that both men and women bring to the classroom. Teachers need to acknowledge the relevance of gender equity. Women have their own unique history, training, and concerns just as men do.

The American Association of University Women ("How Schools Shortchange Girls", 1992) and Bartholomew and Schnorr ("Gender Equity: Educational Problems and Possibilities for Female Students", 1991) suggest some possible strategies for providing an equitable, gender fair education to all females: (1) mentor programs; (2) non-traditional role models; (3) curriculum revisions; (4) curriculum innovation; (5) teacher/counselor training; (6) parental-male peer awareness; (7) mathematics and science course emphasis. Davis, and Nfemiroff (1992) define a gender-fair education as seeking to enable students to develop a critical perspective toward all knowledge, and to empower all students to become equal and active participants in the critical educational process. Davis and Nemiroff critiqued five pedagogical models, such as, (1) "Talking Head" pedagogy, which seeks to reproduce the common wisdom of established knowledge; (2) "Humanistic Education", in which learners and teachers interact to produce knowledge; (3) "Critical Pedagogy", in which teachers and learners produce knowledge through a collective examination of their socio-economic situations; (4) "Early Feminist Pedagogy, which emphasizes the collective production of knowledge, focusing on gender and sexism as universals; (5) "Critical Humanism", which combines the thinking of humanists, critical pedagogues, and feminist educators, and centers the problems of race, social class, ethnicity. These types of strategies would have a major impact in education, if totally implemented.

The quality of life of young people is also effected by gender bias as shown in current research on gender differences in date rape, adolescent violence, adolescent suicide, alcohol and drug

25

abuse, eating disorders, childhood sexual assault, sexual abuse and reasons for dropping out of school (Young, 1992). The research on these issues often provides disturbing messages about women and sends the message that men are eliminated from these social ills. Research on gender and its effects has focused mainly on health concerns, self-concept, achievement and sex roles attitudes, and behavior, but very little on the social implications. Administrators and teachers can no longer look the other way if there is a suspension of sexual harassment. There is very little tolerance for the assumption that "boys will be boys" (Sadker, 1994). Society can no longer encourage aggressive and domineering behavior from males, while asking females to be more accepting of the status quo. Educators need to retrain children against stereotypical thinking and perceptions.

The gender difference in classroom communications is more than a mere counting game of who gets the teacher's attention and who doesn't. Teacher attention is a vote of high expectations and commitment to a student. Decades of research show that seudents who are actively involved in classroom discussion are more likely to achieve and to express positive attitudes toward schools and learning (Flanders, 1970). The reason why some women don't respond in class discussions at the college level is that they are afraid. They often attribute their success to external factors such as luck, rather than to internal factors such as ability (Frieze et. al, 1975). There are trends toward a single sex school setting, but trends in recent times advocate coeducation which is encouraged by such laws as Title IX. A single sex school setting was thought to be beneficial to the achievement of the female student. There are also thoughts that these types of schools would harbor feelings of self-doubt. Questions about capabilities and intellectual competence would be made more evident in single sex schools. Of course, there are exceptions to some of the feelings held by educators and the research indicates variations do exist.

A major, multi-year study of Harvard undergraduates (Light, 1990) supports the claim that women do harbor more self-doubt than men do despite educational achievement, success, or satisfaction. When the Harvard women experience failure, they were quick to doubt themselves. They attributed their problems to self-limitations and personal inadequacies in sharp contrast, their male peers put the blame on others or on circumstances. The Harvard study is powerful when we consider that the gender findings were unanticipated. The Harvard women excelled in academic environments. They were successful in making the grade; they had little experience of academic failure. Yet, these highly

27

intelligent women still carried doubts and questions about their intellectual capabilities. It is believed from this study that a combination of social forces made the women doubt themselves. It is also believed that it is easier for a women to gain approval and attention for their bodies and physical attributes than for the quality of their minds (Light, 1990). The time has come for women to ignore these stereotypes and embrace their femininity.

In conclusion, an African proverb says it takes the whole village to educate a child: this includes grandparents and parents, teachers and school administrators, lawmakers and civil leaders. It will take everyone from our American village join forces; they can transform our educational institutions into the most powerful levers for equity, places where girls are valued as much as boys, daughters are cherished as fully as sons are, and tomorrow's women are prepared to be full partners in all activities of the next century and beyond (Sadker, 1994).

Educators and parents can no longer have their heads buried in the sand. There is a need for equitable education for males as well as females. Society is changing. Everyone needs to be assured that they will have the same opportunities to be all they can be.

BIBLIOGRAPHY

Bigelow, B, Christensen, L. Karp, S., Miner, B., Peterson, B., Levine, D. & Miller, L. (1994). Rethinking Our Classrooms: Teaching For Equity and Justice. Montgomery, AL: Rethinking School, Ltd.

Corelli, A. (1988). Sex Equity in Education. Springfield, IL: Charles C. Thomas, Publisher.

Flanders, N. (1970). Analyzing Teaching Behaviors. Reading, MA: Addison-Wesley.

Gallos, J. V. (1995). Gender and Silence: Implications of Women's Ways of Knowing. College Teaching, 4(13), 101-105.

Klein, Susan S. (1985). Through Education. Baltimore, MA: The Johns Hopkins University Press Handbook for Achieving Sex Equity.

Light, R. (1990). Explorations with students and faculty about teaching, learning, and student life: The first report. Cambridge, MA: The Harvard University Assessment Seminars.

Lord, S. B., Wyman, L., Scott, N. & McLoughlin, X. E. (1979). The Female Experience in America: A Learning/Teaching Guide. Newton, MA: US Department of Health and Welfare.

Manning, M. L. (1993). Cultural and Gender Differnces in Young Adolescents. Middle School Journal,13-17.

29

Noddings, N. (1992). The Gender Issue. Educational Leadership, 65-70.

Rodenstein, Judith M. (1990). Children At Risk: A Resource and Planning Guide. Madison, WI: Wisconsin Department of Public Instruction.

Sadker, Myra & David. (1994). Failing At Fairness: Now America's Schools Cheat Girls. New York, NY: Charles Scribner & Sons.

Sadker, M., Sadker, D., & Long, L. (1993). Gender and Educational Equality. In J. A. Banks & C. A. Banks (Eds.), Multicultural Education: Issues and Perspectives (pp.101-111). Needham, MA: Division of Simon & Schuster, Inc.

Shapira, J., Kramer, S., & Hunerberg, C. (1981). Equal Their Chances: Children's Activities For Non-Sexist Learning. Englewood Cliffs, NJ: Prentice Hall, Inc.

Shashanni, L. (1995). Gender Differences in Mathematics Experiences and Attitude and Their Relation to Computer Attitude. Educational Technology, 35, 32-38.

Tetreault, M. K. T. (1993). Classrooms for Diversity: Rethinking Curriculum and Pedagogy. In J. A. Banks & C. A. Banks (Eds.), Multicultural Education: Issues and perspectives (pp. 111-128). Needham, MA: A division of Simmon & Schuster, Inc.

Young, W. (1992). A-Gay-Yah: A Gender Equity Curriculum For Grades 6-12. Tahlequah, OK: WEEA Publishing Center.

CHAPTER 3

Teachers' Perceptions of the Importance of Multicultural Education in the Classroom

Alice Duhon-Ross, Ph.D.,
Associate Professor
Albany State University
Albany, GA

Angela Battle,
Middle School Teacher
Albany, GA

The twenty-first century has brought about many changes. These changes have caused families to move to different countries, different neighborhoods, and even different schools. The population of the United States is now more diverse, with minority populations increasing in number. Consequently, the student population in the public school system is also changing. The change in population has made multicultural education become a very important topic in the school system. The idea of multicultural education has also brought about much controversy.

In 1976, 24 percent of American public schools were non-white (Pettus & Allain, 1999). It is projected that by the year 2020,

31

the nonwhite population will account for 46 percent of the public school enrollment (Cushner, McClelland, and Stafford; 1992). This change in the diversity of school enrollment has caused things to change. These changes have created what Banks (1998) refers to as the "demographic imperative," a situation that requires classroom practitioners to be more responsive to an increasingly diverse population. The demographic imperative has made it necessary for many schools to provide needed programs to help prepare teachers to effectively instruct students of diverse backgrounds and cultures. Teachers need to be able to teach students to live and function in diverse communities and contribute social prosperity at the national and global levels (Pettus and Allain, 1999).

There are many supporters as well as non-supporters of the concept of multicultural education. The supporters of multicultural education say students must be aware of their own culture and how they are similar and different from others (Noel, 1995). This awareness involves an understanding of issues involving differences in culture and a knowledge of which of these issues are present in the community in which they live. With this goal in mind, teachers become a very important part of the multicultural education component.

"Multicultural education is similar to the pieces of a puzzle. Each piece of a puzzle is different and unique and when they are put together, they form one whole picture. Multicultural education takes its form in the same unique manner. Every member of the society is unique, with different cultural backgrounds, but they all fit together to form one unit" (Noel, 1995).

Multicultural education can be taught in the classroom by using the "puzzle pieces" concept. Since teachers are significant persons in the lives of children, they have a powerful influence on how students' behave. This influence goes beyond the students' behavior. Teachers can also influence students' development of positive or negative attitudes toward their peers regardless of their cultural backgrounds. Meeting the needs of diverse children in the classroom calls for teachers to understand the concept of multicultural education, show sensitivity toward cultural diversity, capitalize on strengths, and avoid accentuating any weaknesses of culturally diverse groups (Irwin, 1999). According to Noel, (1995),

> "...understanding our own identity and the culture of our community requires knowledge and recognition of our culture and communities and how they have shaped us."

Multiculturalism is said to have five dimensions. First is content integration. Content integration occurs when teachers integrate content on different ethnic backgrounds in the curriculum. Second is knowledge construction. Knowledge construction occurs when teachers help students investigate the implicit cultural assumptions and frames of reference of the discipline they're teaching. Third is equity pedagogy. Equity pedagogy involves a change in the methods of teaching used by teachers. This change in the methods of teaching enables kids from diverse racial groups and both genders to achieve. Fourth is prejudice reduction. Prejudice reduction occurs when teachers use different methods of teaching to help kids develop positive racial attitudes. Last is an empowering school structure and social structure. The school and social structure are empowered when teachers and administrators look at the total school structure to see how to make it more equitable (Banks, 1998). These dimensions were developed by Banks to help teachers to understand that multicultural education can be integrated into all subjects.

There are many great ideas to support the multicultural education concept, but there are also arguments against the concept. Some critics believe that "multicultural education is directed toward only minority groups, thus discriminating against middle class, white, heterosexual males. Others believe that multiculturalism is against Western and democratic ideals. A final

34

argument is the claim that multiculturalism will divide our presumably united nation (Banks, 1995).

Multiculturalism as noted in the review of literature is a very important component in the education process. The way a student is taught determines whether or not they learn. When a teacher incorporates multiculturalism into their curriculum, all students are given and equal opportunity to learn. To determine how teachers felt about the concept of multiculturalism, a ten-question survey was developed. The survey that was developed is on the following page.

How Do You Feel About Multicultural Education?

For the purposes of this study, multicultural education refers to equitable education for all students regardless of ethnic and cultural background, gender, race, color, religious affiliation or handicap and implemented to enhance tolerance, respect, understanding, awareness, and acceptance of self and others in the diversity of their cultures. The following is a sample to the study disseminated to area teachers:

Please respond to the following statements based how strongly you agree or disagree with them. Refer to the following scale when marking your answers.

(SA)-Strongly Agree

(A)-Agree

(D)-Disagree

(SD)-Strongly Disagree

1.   Multicultural education is irrelevant where I teach.

2.   It is difficult for me to teach a class of students with varying cultural backgrounds.

3.   I strongly favor multicultural education.

4.   Part of a teacher's job is to make students aware of and tolerant of each other's cultural background.

5.   Training in multicultural education should be provided to all teachers.

6.   Teachers need to understand a student's culture in order to better meet the educational needs of the student.

7.   Multicultural education is a program only for minority students.

8.   Multicultural education should be an integral part of the school curriculum.

9.   Learning about other cultures will help to eliminate

36

10.   Multicultural education should be solely dealt with at home and not at school.

There were thirty surveys sent out. Of the thirty sent out, twenty-three were returned. The information derived from the surveys was surprising. The answers to the surveys were as follows: Many of the responses from the teachers implicated that they were almost split fifty-fifty on how they felt about multicultural issues. All of the teachers, who completed the survey, felt that multiculturalism was important/relevant where they taught. Although the teachers felt that multiculturalism was relevant, only about half of them felt that they would be able to teach students of different backgrounds. Overall, the teachers had mixed feelings toward multiculturalism. Some of the teachers wrote additional comments on their survey. The main issue that was written about was the fact that many of them felt that they could only teach from a multicultural perspective if they were given the proper training. Without the proper training, they felt it would be impossible for them to incorporate it in their curriculum. One teacher wrote the comment that he/she was afraid to teach by using examples of different cultures because they were afraid they might offend some of their students.

When teachers develop a positive attitude about multiculturalism and incorporate it in their curriculum, students of all cultures and backgrounds will be successful. Multiculturalism promotes a positive change for persons of all culture. It not only involves teaching majority groups about minorities, but it also teaches minority groups about the majority groups. If properly incorporated into the curricula, multiculturalism will unite our divided nation into one unit that has no mainstream culture but many diverse subcultures that will work together for the good of all cultures and not just the culture of the majority or minority.

Many high school students were never taught from a perspective that included views of different cultures. Some students acknowledged that what was taught in their high schools was taught from a middle class, white perspective. If students of color are not taught about themselves, their collective cultures, and their surroundings, they cannot be expected to survive in this society. To survive, students must be taught using multicultural concepts to help them to grow and become productive citizens within American society. This survival technique begins with education. Education begins at home and educators continue the process in the classroom.

38

References

Banks, J. (1998). Multiculturalism's five dimensions. NEA Today, 17, 17.

Banks, J. (1995). Multicultural education: Development, dimensions, and challenges. Guilford, CT: The Dushkin Publishing Group.

Cushner, K., McClelland, A., & Safford, P. (1992). Human diversity in education: An integrative approach. New York: McGraw Hill.

Irwin, L. (1999). Do rural and urban teachers differ in their attitudes toward multicultural education? Contemporary Education, 70, 38-43.

Multicultural Pavilion. (2000). Defining multicultural education. [Online].

Noel, J. (1995). Multicultural teacher education: From awareness through emotions to action. Journal of Teacher Education, 46, 267-272.

CHAPTER 4

Sensitizing America on Racism and Discrimination

Michael E. Orok, Ph.D.
Teresa Merriweather-Orok, Ph.D.
Albany State University
Albany, GA

> ...the notion that America's will to racial justice
> is weak and therefore black people must close
> ranks for survival in a hostile country- rests
> principally upon claims to racial authenticity.
> Cornel West, *Race Matters (1993)*

The arrest of an African of Caribbean decent with Rastafarian hairstyle, popularly known as "dread locks" in a Los Angeles suburb several years ago, points to the xenophobic sentiment that permeates the American cultural rationality. It is not uncommon in America to find whites that do not for the most part understand a culture outside their own. Several writings and commentaries have suggested that Africans- hence, African Americans- are savages, cannibalistic and lack a sense of purpose or nationalism. Perhaps the most disturbing element of all of these

41

is the understanding that these same whites appear, at least rhetorically, to subscribe to the pluralistic structure that is supposed to shape American thinking. Despite these racial myths about Native Africans and African Americans, both in America and in the Diaspora, most people in America still uphold that the Constitution was crafted to set the stage for a consistent pluralistic value. The rise of nationalism, Americanism, and so-called "patriotism" soon after World War I only supported the existence of ethnic separatism and ethnic culture. Further, using the Constitution of the United States as a frame of reference, nothing could be farther from the truth if one is to defer from this document that cultural conflict, ethnic hatred, and identity does not dominate American socio-political and economic considerations. In fact, conflicting ideologies abound.

To African Americans in the United States, the story of their racial annihilation by a progressively significant Eurocentric sentiment underscores their contributions to the American society. The dogmatic portrayal of Eurocentric values and the suggestion offered by some that the African Americans must shade all semblance of non-Eurocentric values is in itself racist and discriminatory. While not all African Americans in America are socially sophisticated, economically wealthy, or hold a tremendous number of key strategic positions, it is unarguably true that this population holds the key to America's economic survival. The African-American contributions to advancements in science, medicine, engineering, government and the legal professions are no less significant than those of any other group. In America, out of its racist orientation, Native Africans and African Americans can expect to be called names like *Tarzan, Kunte Kinte*, etc.; be kept waiting hours for appointments, and are disproportionately denied access to economic opportunities that other groups take for granted. Some of their books dealing with African political propaganda have been banned and their scholarly articles are refused publications in major journals. Their technical offerings are viewed with cool disdain. As for the Native Africans, their accents and writing styles are often mocked.

Discrimination involves the isolation of the African American by the white dominant group even within small groups. It can be directly or indirectly institutionalized. Many African Americans cannot in a direct way access some of the country clubs and social groups that exist in the United States. As a Native African, one of my most memorable racist encounters took place over fifteen years ago. I was employed in a small restaurant in Ohio where the management thought that my skills were not adequate as a cook even though I had worked there for at least a year. I noticed that new hires regardless of their infantile demeanor were responsible for food preparation and serving immediately upon employment. Within two years, I was assigned to floor sweeping, restroom cleaning, and dishwashing under a white manager. It took the subsequent employment of an African American manager to change my condition. It was he who explained to me why my condition had not changed. Out of the continent of Africa and having been in the United States only two years, I was naive enough to believe all of the propaganda about how America was the land of the brave and that freedom and fairness was unlimited.

It never occurred to me that the white community saw me as a jungle animal that did not yet embrace civilization and was unable to talk about food preparation that was sufficient for American consumption. The African American manager did assign me as a short order cook and I became the best short order cook they ever had. That was fifteen years ago and for me the situation has not improved. I am faced with subtle situations daily. On a daily basis, I notice Caucasians, especially women grabbing their purses and pulling them closer to their persons while in front of me at a store counter or doing likewise with their children when

I approach, especially when I am in street clothes. In my suit and tie, I am more likely to be addressed as a sir. Assuming that when properly attired, I am more likely to behave differently.

Occasionally, my wife shares a story or two with me about her encounters with racism in America as an African American person born and raised in Tennessee. Having been born during the 1960's and reared in a rural community bought many challenges for her. First, the public school was segregated and unequally funded to provide African-American students with out-dated books and materials. She remembers her first grade teacher, Mrs. Iola Brocks, as a strong and committed educator who enabled her students to have their first opportunities to engage in cultural arts. Mrs. Brocks was an avid novice playwright who constructed handmade costumes from paper bags and heavily dyed tissue paper.

My wife's elementary school provided education for youth in grades one through eight. After desegregation of public schools occurred in the mid-1960's, she and her classmates were bused to a school about 10 miles from home and anticipated that White students would join with them to pursue educational opportunities. To their limited wisdom and brevity in conceptualizing racism in America, they were joined only by those few Whites who could not afford the transportation to schools located in "town". Despite efforts of desegregation, she continued to witness acts of racism, over and over again in her life. After graduating from high school, she enrolled at Lane College, in Jackson, Tennessee. There her understanding of racism was broadened and she began to understand the impact of those racial issues that divided and continue to divide our society. The perception held by most Whites in the town about Lane College centered on students being ill prepared and unequipped to deal with life issues.

Despite efforts to minimize African-American educational opportunities, my wife's strongest ethical and moral values have been acquired in these less than aesthetically pleasing buildings. Historically black colleges and universities continue to serve a pivotal role in providing education for African-Americans. Although we have made significant strides, the battle has not be won. Educational institutions have not addressed the issue of racism in a different way. Most white teachers belief that African American children are incapable of learning, therefore they continuously award them poor grades. In many southern states, the incident of tracking is properly documented. African American children are encouraged by their high school advisers to select the general diploma tract as opposed to the college preparatory or vocational tracts as a result, many never earn the requisite credits or passed the courses required for college admissions. Those who enter college are faced with racial abuses by white faculty who do not still belief in their capabilities. I teach at a small historically black university and I hear complains by African American students about Caucasian faculty members who do not belief in their capabilities and some even shun the idea of an African American administrator being their supervisor.

A friend even pointed out the other day about how his American (naturalized) citizenship is often viewed as a hoax and less patriotic than those of European decent. In his experience, he elaborated on how an immigration officer at one United States airport opened his American passport and spent more than ten minutes examining the document and his photograph while others of non-African decent continuously left the screening site without delay. From a broader perspective, the picture of the dominant group and their inseparable political, economic and social environments and their intentional and non-intentional practices and "a mixture of prejudice and racism is what Feagan calls systematic discrimination." The argument can be advanced another way. A question can be posed thus- "When Euro cultural supremacy and those who postulate such, challenge or abuse the

47

Native African, the African American and their culture, does it in fact underscore their intellectual development or achievement in the United States?"

Not so. In fact, over the past three centuries, Africans everywhere have been conditioned by slavery. They have been subjected to western civilization and brainwashed to regard themselves as inferior and negative people.

But this is an oxymoron, because all along the African mind had been liberated. Africa has witnessed the intellectual engineering of ideas of such American-trained nationalist like Nigeria's Nnamdi Azikiwe and other European-trained individuals such as Ghana's Kwame Nkrumah.

Other Africans such as Tanzania's Julius Nyerere have had a significant impact on policies outside Africa. Their efforts parallel those of their African American counterparts such as Dr. Martin Luther King, Jr., W.E.B. DuBois and Malcolm X among others.

Even with these achievements, Native African and African Americans still feel small and the attempt by White society to alienate them is a constant reminder of their assigned place in society. In fact, the white individual gets irritated at their familiarity with the American socio-political and economic system.

When Malcom X spoke of white racism, he refused to compromise on the devaluation of the African American life. So was Julius Nyerere when he amplified the slogan "Africa must be free." He was not only talking about freedom from foreign rule. His cry for freedom extended to all men and women of African decent, both in and out of Africa. He meant freedom for all forms of oppression, which includes racism and discrimination. It is therefore ridiculous to find a country such as the United States of America with its expression of democracy that calls for complete unity of all its people to voluntarily discriminate and racially invalidate the importance of one of its many groups.

America must search her soul and make a serious effort to eliminate or at least minimize the ferocity that has been placed on Africans in the United States if our diverse culture is to mean anything for our future growth and development. The contributions of African Americans to this society must be recognized and all forms of prejudice, racial overtones and discriminatory activities must be minimized in order that groups can develop the willingness to work for the good of our society.

REFERENCES

Brink, W., & Harris, L. (1964). The Negro Revolution in America. New York: Simon and Schuster

Kitano, H. H. L. (1991). Race Relations (4th Edition). New Jersey: Prentice Hall.

Lynch, H. (1978). Black Africa Set 1, Vol. 5 New York: Arno Press

Schwartz, M. A. (1967). Trends in White Attitudes Toward Negroes. Chicago: National Opinion Research Center

West, C. (1993). Race Matters. New York: Vintage Books.

CHAPTER 5

Fun House Mirrors:
At-Promise vs. At-Risk Perceptions of Urban Students

Nanthalia W. McJamerson, Ph. D.
Grambling State University
Grambling, LA

When students see their reflections in the eyes of teachers who have negative visions of them, it is no wonder so many see themselves as headed for problems rather than possibilities. The "at-risk" label and resulting schooling practices have been prevalent with urban students.

According to Swadener and Lubeck (1995), there is a need to change the discourse about students "at-risk" to discourse about students "at promise". Many resilience researchers and educators (Werner, 1996; Wolin and Wolin, 1993) advocate classroom approaches which will move students from risk to resilience characterization. In this chapter, an autobiography project is presented as one classroom approach to turning the process of schooling toward an emphasis on student promise and the potential for success.

Among the classroom approaches recommended (Swandener and Lubeck, 1995) for the transformation from risk to resilience are: (1) Teach to students' strengths, (2) Teach students that they have innate resilience, (3) Provide growth opportunities for students, (4) Create opportunities for students to participate and contribute personal strengths.

In order to change future teachers' perceptions of youth from at-risk to at-promise, I engage them in autobiographical studies. The study of success complies with the recommendation to "teach students that they have innate resilience". Furthermore, when used with preservice teachers, it teaches them that their future students will possess innate resilience.

In Phase I of the autobiographical studies, the emphasis is placed on the direct experience of empowerment for teachers and counselors in training. Phase II is focused on the changes in the perceptions of the preservice teachers regarding their future students, which is the first step in the turn toward fostering resilience and excellence.

Phase I

The work of demystifying success through the "RECONSTRUCTING" Lives Project began in 1991 as four graduate counseling majors at South Carolina State University

52

diligently searched for those factors which transformed persons who faced extraordinary obstacles into persons with extraordinary achievements in their lives. Their worked produced a "Success Fibers Model of Development" based on their discovery of six essential factors or common fibers in the lives of achievers: (1) Ability Nurture, (2) Ambition Ignition, (3) Cardiac Reserve, (4) Competency Training, (5) Opportunity Ramrods and (6) Insight Dividends (McJamerson, N., 1998).

Subjects

Fifty-one undergraduate teaching majors participated in a "RECONSTRUCTING" Lives Project, studying the life of Dr. Benjamin Carson through the study of his autobiography, *Gifted Hands*. As part of the educational psychology course offered in the department, students were divided into seven groups. All groups were engaged in the following procedures.

First, participants identified, analyzed and evaluated critical, transformative factors, which led to the achiever's eventual success. Specifically, participants described and illuminated particular behaviors, strategies, knowledge and types of experience, which made a difference in achieving goals and overcoming limitations and challenges.

53

Second, participants were engaged in the creative process of "reconstructing" the achiever's life by removing success factors and speculating about what that person might have become without the respective factors. The critical teaching nature of the project was enhanced with the task of creating skits to depict the "reconstructed" life by each group (Shor, 1987, 1992).

Methods

The effects of the "RECONSTRUCTING" Lives Project approach were ascertained from observation-participation throughout a four-week period of group work. The second method used was an open-ended survey which required a written response to the question, "How did the "RECONSTRUCTING" Lives Project affect you?"

Results

Observations showed that students discovered and discussed similarities between their own struggles and strengths and those of successful persons, and they, subsequently, analyzed their own behavior regarding success. Furthermore, rather than merely admire or stand in awe of famous persons, participants expressed the possibilities of creating transformations in their lives (McJamerson, N., 2000). On the survey used to determine the

54

impact of the "Reconstructing" Lives Project, fifty out of fifty-one participants reported the development of a sense of empowerment in four categories: (1) increased insight; (2) increased encouragement; (3) new awareness of possibilities for personal success and (4) actual behavior changes and plan for behavior changes to create personal success (McJamerson, 1998).

Phase II

During the Spring 2000 semester, thirty-two teaching majors were engaged in the Reconstructing Lives Project with the additional task of explaining the lessons they learned regarding becoming teachers. Three major themes emerged: (1) Some of the developmental theories seem to be accurate in their claims that the environment has powerful effects on academic and personal achievement, (2) Teachers can make a critical difference in students' lives, (3) They will not "look at" children in the same way in the future, as "you never know what a child can become". Those results indicate that the goal of changing future teachers' perceptions was achieved.

Conclusion

The *"RECONSTRUCTING"* Lives Project was described as a positive and powerful experience, in which persons develop a sense of empowerment for creating success in their own and in others' lives. Such work can provide insight for teachers, counselors, parents and policy makers for developing human potential.

REFERENCES

Berlak, A. and Berlak, H. (1981). The Dilemmas of Schooling. London: Methuen.

Beyer, L.E. (1979). Schools, Aesthetic Forms, and Social Reproduction. Madison: University of Wisconsin.

Carson, B. and Murphey, C. (1990). Gifted Hands. Grand Rapids, MI: Zondervan Publishing House.

Freire, P. (1973). Pedagogy of the Oppressed. New York: Seabury.

Giroux, H. A. (1978). Writing and Critical Thinking in the Social Studies. Curriculum Inquiry, 8(1), 291-310.

Glaser, B. and Strauss, A. (1976). The Discovery of Grounded Theory: Strategies for Qualitative Research. Chicago: Aldine.

Hale, J. (1994). Unbank the Fire: Visions for the Education of African American Children. Baltimore: The Johns Hopkins University Press.

McJamerson, J. (1999). On the Shoulders of Our Ancestors: African American History Through Poetic Verse. Ruston, LA: Washington Wings Empowerment Group.

McJamerson, N. (2000). "'Reconstructing' Lives: A Reading-for-Empowerment Project". In G. Duhon-Boudreaux

(Ed.), An Interdisciplinary Approach to Issues and Practices in Teacher Education. New York: The Edwin Mellen Press.

Pardeck, J. T. & Pardeck, J. A. (1989). "Bibliotherapy: Does It Work?" Journal of Counseling and Development, 67 (9).

Shor, I. (1992). Empowering Education: Critical Teaching for Social Change. Chicago: University of Chicago Press.

Swadener, B., & Lubeck, S. (Eds.). (1995). Children and Families "At Promise": Deconstructing the Discourse of Risk. Albany, NY: State University of New York Press.

Werner, E. (1996). "How Kids Become Resilient: Observations and Cautions." Resiliency in Action, 1(1), 18-28.

Wolin, S. J. and Wolin, S. (1993). The Resilient Self: How Survivors of Troubled Families Rise Above Adversity. New York: Villard Books.

Woodson, C. G. (1990). The Mis-Education of the Negro. Trenton, NJ: African World Press (Original work published 1933).

CHAPTER 6

I Am "Bad, "And You Can 't Stop Me

Jimmy McJamerson, M.A. +30
Grambling State University
Grambling, LA

Historical Note

The first poem activity is centered around *I Am "Bad, "And You Can't Stop Me.* This particular poem was written especially for our youth and anyone who needs to be motivated to say very clearly that, regardless of the negative images which surround you, you can excel. To excel is as easy as breathing, especially if you decide that nothing can deter you from achieving. Our ancestral heritage fills us with pride and tells us that we can excel when we try. *I Am "Bad," And You Can't Stop Me* is the essence of the entire workbook because it reminds one of past achievements and motivates one to action, to get up and move, to try again and to set your sight for the horizon and not the valleys in life.

I Am "Bad," And You Can't Stop Me

I shall, I will excel because I am bad, and you can't stop me. I read everything because knowledge is power. In math, Pythagorean theorem is as easy as 1, 2, 3. I can recite the poetry of Nikki Giovanni with ease, and I can play Beethoven's 5th Symphony with the fortitude of my being. You see, I am naturally gifted that way, for I am bad, and you can't stop me.

I can run with the best runners, keeping stride with Flo Jo and Carl Lewis. I can soar with the eagles like Michael Jordan when he puts on his show, for I am bad and you can't stop me.

I can achieve, and I will achieve. My inspiration comes from the Nubian Queen- Tiye; Bilal- the Islamic cryer; Kunta Kinte- who rejected slavery; Phyillis Wheatley- the first African-American poetist; Joe Louis- the "Brown Bomber"; Barbara Jordan- the Superb warrior/lawyer; Marva Collins- the ultimate teacher; Sammy Davis, Jr.- the master showman; Dr. M. L. King- the supreme leader; and Jesse Jackson- the master politician. For I am bad, and you can't stop me.

I can be humble as George Washington Carver or as shrewd as Booker T. Washington or as "deep" as Malcolm X. I am bad, and you can't stop me.

No drug pusher nor pimp can stop me; no racism, nor bigotry, nor injustice; for I am bad and you can't stop me.

Like "Ice-T", I use my mind for a lethal weapon and like B. D. P. (Boogie Down Productions), I shall never forget my history, for I am bad, and you can't stop me.

60

Like Muhammed Ali, who declared, "I am the greatest", I now declare, I am bad, and you can't stop me!

(Dedicated to Ms. Nicole Tian McJamerson, my daughter, you are "Bad")
Jimmy McJamerson, 1990

Poem Title: *I Am "Bad, " And You Can 't Stop Me*

Activities

Directions
Read the poem twice and then complete the activities listed below.

Definitions
Define the following terms in 1 or 2 sentences. Students may use a dictionary, if necessary.

1.	excel	6.	inspiration	11.	humble
2.	Pythagorean Theorem	7.	crier	12.	shrewd
3.	"bad"	8.	master politician	13.	bigotry
4.	soar	9.	neurosurgeon	14.	"deep"
5.	lethal weapon	10.	masonic	15.	stride

Identification

Identify the following persons by selecting three to five on which to write a one-page essay. Explain why each person should be remembered. Students must cite their sources.

1. Nikki Giovanni   11. Marva Collins

2. Beethoven   12. Sammy Davis, Jr.

3. Flo Jo   13. Dr. M. L. King, Jr.

4. Carl Lewis   14. Prince Hall

5. Michael Jordan   15. Jesse Jackson

6. Nubian Queen Tiye   16. John Johnson

7.   Kunta Kinte   17. Dr. Daniel Hale Williams

8. Phyllis Wheatley   18. Dr. Benjamin Carson

9. Joe Louis   19. George Washington Carver

10. Barbara Jordan   20. Malcolm X

Multiple Choice

Place the letter of the correct answer in the blank before the number.

1. One of the poets discussed in this poem is

    a.   Maya Angelou   c.   Nikki Giovanni

    b.   Bill Cosby   d.   Malcolm X

2.   Which of the following persons is described as being
      clever, thus outwitting others?

      a. George Washington Carver   c. Dr. M. L. King, Jr.

      d. Booker T. Washington   b. Sammy Davis, Jr.

3.   Which of the following will not deter a person as discussed
      in this selection?

      a.   a lethal weapon   c. master politician

      b.   slavery   d. drug pusher

4.   From your study, which one of the following conducted
      research using the peanut?

      a. Dr. Benjamin Carson   c. Booker T. Washington

      b. George Washington Carverd. Dr. Daniel Hale Williams

5.   Who authored *Gifted Hands?*

      a. Dr. Daniel Hale Williams c. Nikki Giovanni

      b. John Johnson   d. Dr. Benjamin Carson

<u>Essay</u>

Answer the following questions in essay format:

1.   What does this poem mean to you?

2.   Why should African-Americans or anyone else want to adhere to the principles outlined in this work?

3.   Who was Booker T. Washington and why should his contributions to American society be remembered?

4.   What are *Ebony,* and *Jet?* What is the meaning of each term?

5.   Dr. Benjamin Carson authored how many books, and what are their titles? Have you read any of his books?

<u>In-Class Activity</u>

Have each student re-read paragraph three (3) which begins with "I can achieve, and I will achieve..." After completing this task, have them replace the names of the individuals with the names of other Africans and/or African-Americans. For example:

"My inspiration comes from the Egyptian Queen Isis."

Homework

After each student completes the activity described in In-Class Activity, have each read aloud what he or she has written. Using the best responses, have the whole class write a similar poem. Reproduce the finished poem and give each student a copy. Also, have the class fill out a copyright form and mail it.

CHAPTER 7

I Am A Teacher

Jimmy McJamerson, M.A. +30
Grambling State University
Grambling, LA

Historical Note

The noble role of the teacher has not been valued as much as other occupations in American society. Many teachers, whether professionally trained for the classroom or personally teaching by example, are truly the molders and shapers of our future. In African-American society prior to the 1960s, the teaching profession was one of the few occupations African-Americans were encouraged to join. This profession is still one of the noblest ones of all times. African-Americans who were newly elected to the various state legislatures during the Reconstruction Period were the first to establish free universal education for all Americans regardless of their economic status. *I Am A Teacher* celebrates the tradition of teaching.

I Am A Teacher

I am a teacher because I dream of a better world, where people are more important than material possessions. I will always foster the dignity and individuality of those in my charge.

Through my actions and deeds, I shall instill pride, respect, honesty and the thirst for knowledge. I am a teacher, and I am proud of it.

I shall always encourage my students to learn- even those who are not willing- and I shall demand that they do their best at all times.

As a teacher, I shall not impose my thoughts and ideas upon my students. I will always strive to create an environment open for discussion, analysis and differing opinions.

I realize that I am a shaper and molder of the future; I cherish the precious minds in my charge.

You see, I am a teacher, and I am proud of it.
Jimmy McJamerson, 1990.

Poem Title: *I Am A Teacher*

Activities

Directions
Read the poem twice and then complete the activities listed below.

Definition
Define the following terms in 1 or 2 sentences. Students may use a dictionary or other resource materials, if necessary.

1.	foster	6.	encourage
2.	dignity	7.	inspire
3.	individuality	8.	strive
4.	deeds	9.	analysis
5.	honesty	10.	inspiration

Discussion items
Explain in your own words what the following concepts mean.

1.	teacher	5.	honesty
2.	material	6.	dream of a better world
3.	thirst for knowledge	7.	dignity and individuality
4.	differing opinion	8.	precious minds in my charge

Completion

Complete the following sentences taken from the poem.

1.   I am a teacher because I _____.

2.   Where people are more important than _____.

3.   I am a teacher, and I _____.

4.   I cherish the precious minds _____.

5.   I will always strive to create an environment open for ____,

        _____ and _____ .

In-Class Activity

After the students have completed the homework assignment, have them then plan a reception or program in which each student will present a copy of the autobiography to their selective teacher.

Homework

Have each student to select a teacher of their choice and write a 2 to 3 page biographical sketch focusing on why they became teachers. Students will have to interview each teacher once permission has been granted.

CHAPTER 8

To Pass or Not to Pass: That is the Question

Mary M Addison, Ed. D.
Dolores A. Westmoreland, Ed. D.
Houston Independent School District
Houston, TX

> *Those who do not remember the past are condemned to relive it.*
> George Santayana, The Life of Reason (1905-06), 459.

> *What so tedious as a twice-told tale?*
> Homer, Odyssey (9th c. B.C.).

The above quotations represent divergent opinions regarding the retention or promotion of the at-risk student. Educational personnel supporting retention might cite the first quotation as a mantra for their cause while the second quotation would be the motto of those bearing the social promotion standard.

To explore this question, this chapter will review the historical perspectives, which have been fundamental in determining the present-day attitudes regarding retention decisions. Theoretical philosophies, which have influenced the conceptual fabric of retention ideology, are next explored. Academic attitudes

71

regarding retention, which identify a given campus's response to unproductive students, are next examined. The characteristics of the retained student as evidenced through research are then presented with student perceptions regarding retention being discussed. Empirical findings concerning retention are reported and conclusions which might be drawn from the preceding sections given.

Historical Perspectives

In 1847, John D. Philbrick introduced a system of education, which was to become the model for the present educational plan: the graded school. The Philbrick model had two distinguishing characteristics. The first was a sequentially arranged curriculum, which allowed student mastery in an augmentative power of difficulty. Secondly, teachers with a system began to concentrate upon a specific area of the curriculum. When it was determined that a student had become competent in a given grade, he was allowed to progress to the succeeding one. The public hailed Philbrick's model as an educational elixir for the student population of the era for such reasons as:

1.   The homogenous grouping of students allowed effortless instruction.

2. Homogeneously grouped students were perceived to prompt fewer discipline problems.

3. Homogeneously grouped students would permit a higher pupil-teacher ratio in each classroom.

4. Teachers of homogeneously grouped students were thought to require less formal training, thus demanding less monetary compensation for their skills.

Student evaluation was the result of two opposing influential references upon the schools—cultural and organizational. Because the schools were expected to be scholarly, financially, and socially efficient, instructionally, the previous specialized, individualized lessons were abandoned in favor of mass synchronous group instruction. With this methodology, it was expected that, as the whole class learned a given lesson, they could then proceed, as a group entity, to more difficult topics.

Culturally, the schools were expected to instill a meritorious value system, which rewards independent effort and ability resulting in earned inequality. In other words, the student ascended to the next level of instruction based upon his own initiative and ability.

It can be seen in an attempt to resolve how the two divergent premises, group aspirations versus individual

73

achievement, would embrace one of three strategies of student evaluation:

1. *Social promotion.* With this strategy, the entire class was allowed to advance to the next grade level without consideration of individual achievement.

2. *Tracking.* This was a compromise strategy between the two premises whereby students were identified, according to ability, into groups. Once classified, the members within the group could be socially promoted or subjected to promotional standards determined by ability. In this strategy, the curricula are adapted to the abilities of the group being served.

3. *Merit Promotion.* This strategy emphasized individual achievement rather than group aspirations and the student must adapt to the curricula being presented.

Nineteenth century public schools favored the third strategy for their classified students. Unfortunately, because the instruction was designed to accommodate the majority of the student body whose abilities were located in the center of the intellectual continuum, it soon became apparent that some members within a given grade would not certify for entrance into the next grade level.

Non-achievers were required to repeat the entire grade because the curricula contained no provisions for remediation in specific subjects (Hess, 1978). Additionally, educators theorized that repeated exposure to the essential elements until mastery by the non-productive students was mandatory (Labaree, 1999).

In the 1870s, the policy of grade retention came under attack by William T. Harris. An innovative and influential superintendent of schools in St. Louis, Missouri, Harris argued that the current graded system did not satisfy the students within divergent positions on the educational ability continuum: the accelerated and the basic student. He believed that the system encouraged school dropouts by forced repetition of an entire year of schooling. Harris implemented a system of quarterly promotions, which allowed early advancement to the next grade upon successful completion of the required examinations. Harris the curriculum was designed to address student diversities organized ability groups within the same classroom.

The high school students of the Roaring Twenties were subject to a change in retention policy. Instead of having to repeat an entire year in high school, they were allowed to repeat only the subject in whom they were deficient. Scholars in the Depression era were introduced to a new concept regarding educational

75

placement: *social promotion.* Proponents of the new arrangement in scholastic determination cited as their rationale that social promotion would permit students to remain in school, thus, affording adults the opportunity to attain the paucity of employment opportunities available during that time of economic crisis. Additionally, proponents of social promotion argued that retaining a student did not improve his academic status, but discriminated against the below average and unwilling student.

With the emphasis upon social promotion rather than merit promotion, the attitude paradigm of the school changed:

-from a goal of individual selection to a goal of group learning;

-from an assumption of differential capability to an assumption of equal capability;

-from a concern with adapting the student to the school to a concern with adapting the school to the student;

-from a focus upon the best students to a focus upon the average student;

-from a fear of precocity (underageness) to a fear of retardation (overageness);

-from an emphasis on testing to an emphasis on certification. (Labaree, 1999).

Social promotion practices reached its zenith during the 1970s when it was estimated that 90% of the nation's schools were practicing the policy. Within the last thirty years the validity of social promotion has been challenged as schools are being accredited based upon quantitative test results. With the social promotion option being diminished, retention has remained the primary solution for academic insufficiency.

Theoretical Philosophies

The thesis for retention could have evolved from several theoretical premises. Jean Piaget, the Swiss psychologist, introduced his unique theory of cognitive functional development in the 1920s. Piaget categorized child development into four hierarchical stages, with each stage having an approximate age parameter. Piaget's theory posits that individual differences in growth rate have allowed variances in the academic achievement of same age students (Carstens, 1985). When students have not internalized the thought processes required to complete successfully a specific educational objective, they should be retained until such internalization has been accomplished. Promoting a youngster who has not acquired the necessary mentations will result in continued academic inadequacies.

77

It is Andrea Carstens' (1985, p. 55) conviction that "the Gesellian theory of development (1928) is the only framework which openly addresses and recommends retention." This philosophy is predicated upon the belief of behavior being the function of growth that "is structured, orderly, predictable, and measurable" (May & Welch, 1984, p. 381). Arnold Gesell, a medical doctor, espoused his theory of development after years of studying infants and preschool children. One of Gesell's (1974, p. 6) favorite sayings, "the mind manifests itself," was interpreted to mean that the actions of an infant or child were the external manifestations of the child's mind. Louise Ames (1981, p. 36), Associate Director of the Gesell Institute, has explained, "we feel children should start school—and subsequently be promoted—on the basis of their behavior age, rather than on the basis of their age in years or their I.Q." Citing "a slight and temporary hurt would be worth it if retention resulted in the child's being placed in a grade where he could be comfortable and could do the work," (Ames (1981, p. 36) encouraged parents to avoid the over-placement of children into untenable situations.

B. F. Skinner's (1938) theory of conditioned behavior has received much discussion with respect to the retention and social promotion of students. Skinner has argued that behavioral conditioning did, indeed, exist in education since "teachers have conditioned students to sit up straight and to be quiet through looks, grades, and physical punishment" (Ozmon & Carver, p. 212). Skinner viewed learning to be hierarchical and believed the teacher's task was to direct students through a series of cognitive sequences reinforced by rewards which would culminate with the acquisition of mastery of predetermined skill. Socially promoting a student who had not achieved proficiency in the requisite basic skills, in effect, preordained his failure. Conversely, requiring a retained student to repeat hierarchical skills already mastered often resulted in apathy and misbehavior.

These developmental theories of learning have served as a catalyst to initiate debate regarding the retention of students.

Academic Attitudes

Examination of permanent school records would likely disclose the prevailing philosophy regarding retention or placement of students at a given school. A high percentage of student body retentions or placements, for example, would probably imply a philosophical assent for that policy. Since the inception of each practice, arguments have been postulated in defense of the favored action.

79

The decisions to retain a student who had not demonstrated the necessary grade proficiencies have been predicated upon many of the following premises:

1.   All students can learn and have been endowed with an innate ability for educational success.

2.   The student, not the instructor has the accountability for curriculum mastery. (Balow & Schwager, 1990).

3.   The curriculum for each grade level is pertinent for all students enrolled in that grade level.

4.   There exist a divergence between successive grade levels which necessitated student mastery of essential elements prior to advancement (McAfee, 1981).

5.   Students promoted without sufficient mastery of the essential elements would impede the class progress and would cast a negative reflection upon the teacher who recommended their promotion (Miller, Frazier, and Richey, 1980).

6.   Since every school is mandated to instill a modicum of responsibility, students deficient academically must accept the inevitability of retention (Schwager & Balow, 1990).

7.   Promotion of students with unqualified academic

records detracts from the efforts of those who earned a legitimate promotion.

8. Most students, having an essential elemental deficit, would experience psychological awkwardness when placed interaction with their prepared class members (Walker, 1984).

9. Students perceived as immature would profit from a year of social, physical and intellectual maturation in the same grade level.

10. Students retained could be located in more homogeneous academic environments, which would be conducive to optimum learning conditions.

11. The possibility of retention could serve as a motivational catalyst for learning success.

Advocating the automatic promotion of students, behaviorists have argued vehemently against the retention of students, utilizing many of the following rationales:

1. The plurality of students retained has not evidenced academic improvement.

2. Retention lessened student's self-concept which could negatively impact student's achievement.

3. Individual differences exhibited by students in

81

assimilation of information have not been addressed by retention.

4. Achievement tests, used to determine student proficiency, may be biased and unreliable.

5. Retention practices may be punitive toward minority and special-population students.

6. Homogeneous grouping of retained students did not provide motivation for academic achievement.

7. The retained student has been placed in a position of academic pursuit with his promoted peers.

8. Retention has not appeared to reduce the divergence of abilities within a given classroom.

9. A positive relationship has been established between retention and failure to complete schooling (Schuyler, 1986).

10. A positive relationship has been established between retention and delinquency.

11. A majority of retained students in a given class reduce the educational level and work productivity of the class.

On the other hand, retention advocates have frequently postulated the following as rebuttal arguments against social promotion:

1. Social promotion has instilled a spurious impression of achievement (Ebel, 1980).

2. Motivational incentives for academic mastery has been diminished by social promotion.

3. Teachers have expressed lower academic expectations for socially promoted students.

4. Socially promoted students have been graduated lacking the necessary social and cognitive skills for effective societal assimilation.

5. The educational progress of the classroom have often been interrupted by the deportment of socially promoted students.

6. Social promotion has produced attitudes of apathy, learned helplessness and inadequacy (Harness, 1984).

7. Socially promoted students are often disturbing influences upon other students in the classroom.

8. Social promotion places the burden of educational failure upon the student alone.

9. Teachers do not accept accountability for the

students who are expected to be socially
promoted regardless of academic achievement.

10.   Socially promoted students face the possibility
of becoming a school drop out because of
escalating problems.

Needless to say, each philosophy has its advocates who
have cited justification for their position and who have
enumerated, from their perspectives, legitimate arguments against
the opposing view.   When arguments for both philosophies are
examined, it is interesting to note the similarities claimed by each
against the other:

1.   Both are thought to damage the students' self-concept.

2.   Both are found to penalize specific groups of students.

3.   Both place an unfair burden upon the students to master
the curriculum alone.

4.   Both are thought to lower the school's academic standards.

5.   Both are thought to increase discipline problems.

6.   Both do not assist students academically.

7.   Both place a responsibility burden upon the instructors.

8.   Both have a positive correlation with truancy, delinquency,
and dropout rates.

Renaissance of Merit Promotion

With the publication of *A Nation at Risk* in 1983, the public denounced social promotion as the *root of all academic achievement evil*. Social promotion was believed to be responsible for the decline in standardized achievement examination scores, especially college-entrance exams, the SAT and the ACT. Additionally, several lawsuits had been initiated when parents believed that their offspring were allowed to graduate from high school being functionally illiterate.

As the academic pendulum moved in the direction of more stringent promotional standards, the emergence of four educational plans were seen:

1.   *Back to Basics*   Proponents of this plan advocate reducing the number of elective courses being taught in all the grades and increasing the amount of time spent on the core curriculum of reading, writing, science, mathematics, and social studies.   Under this plan, children in elementary school would have little time to spend on such subjects as art, music, or physical education, but would have additional training in remedial reading and/or mathematics.   At the secondary level, in addition to those enumerated elementary electives, course offerings such as vocational agriculture,

home economics, and industrial technology would be replaced with additional offerings categorized as *academic solids.*

2.   *Minimum Competency Testing*   To justify the merit promotion being imposed, school systems embraced standardized testing as the benchmark for promotion. Additionally, because the public is able to understand statistics being presented, the test results were used to demonstrate school accountability.   Standardized tests would be sought which emphasized the minimum competencies for next-grade entrance or high school graduation.

3.   *Retention*   Under the new regime of competency examinations, students who failed to demonstrate minimum competency, by virtue of having failed the test being administered, were retained in their present grade.   School districts across the nation have not demonstrated consistency with regard to the criterion being examined on the standardized examinations nor the amount of reliance being placed upon the examination results, themselves, as a basis for retention.

4.   *Remediation*   Most school districts have implemented an

aggressive program of remediation designed to .assist retained students in achieving promotional status.

School Paradigm Shift

The introduction of merit promotion produced attitudinal changes in the philosophy of public schools:

1. A greater concern was given to student merit than to group efficiency.

2. The focus upon collective learning was replaced with individual achievement.

3. Students, previously perceived as having homogeneous abilities, were seen to demonstrate heterogeneous abilities.

4. Instead of adapting the school curricula to the student; the student was forced to adapt to the rigid curricula of the school.

5. The emphasis was changed from the average student to the poorest student.

6. The concern regarding over-aged students was shifted to concern about the under-achieving student.

7. The requirement of certification as the criterion for promotion was changed to the requirement of exit testing.

Promotion versus Retention Empirical Research

The preponderance of research conducted regarding retention since the 1970s has been in the area of achievement and has followed the taxonomy of Jackson (1975) who classified the studies into three categories or types.

The Type I study is a comparison of retained students with promoted students. Researchers have attempted to match the two groups under consideration using such characteristics as sex, grade level, chronological and/or mental age, I.Q., academic and/or achievement results, and socioeconomic factors. This research was considered biased in favor of promotion because the retained student evidently was experiencing some aspect of difficulty or he would have been promoted. Wright (1979) examining forty-five retained first-grade students with an equal number of promoted students and controlling for age differences, found no significant difference in achievement existed, although a numerical advantage appeared among retained students in terms of achievement. She remarked that "it is not likely that the impact on achievement of grade retention for these children was great enough to justify its use in these cases." (1981, p. 3418A).

A two-year study conducted by Nicklason on students from two large Utah school districts sharing different philosophical

88

viewpoints regarding retention indicated no significant differences existed between the two groups in verbal intellectual ability or in academic achievement, however, the promoted pupils were found to affirm a significantly greater growth pattern in the area of reading achievement than were their retained classmates. In the areas of arithmetic achievement, personal adjustment, or social adjustment, Nicklason found no statistical differences. This led to her surmise that the results of her study supported the suppositions that retention neither achieved its assumed goals of increased student achievement nor of personal or social achievement. Studies by Holmes (1986), McDaid (1987), and Yoshida (1989) supported Nicklason's findings regarding retained students' achievement when compared to their promoted peers. Consequently, the authors have stated that the belief held by many educators that a full year's retention in a class will boost academic achievement or self-concept has not been borne by empirical research.

Divergent research results were observed by Oldham (1982), Gutierrez (1982), and Peterson (1983) demonstrated that retained students significantly out-performed their promoted duplicates during the first year following retention as well as in the year during retention. These researchers concluded that the results did not indicate that retention is harmful academically as other studies had found.

Kerzner (1982) selected the records of students in grades one through five who had been retained and who had completed a year of schooling beyond the retention year. Statistical analysis revealed that the retained students experienced any achievement gains. This led the author to surmise that retention in the lower three grades is beneficial.

Contrary to Kerzner's findings, studies conducted upon students who had been retained in grades one through eight by Walker and Madhere (1987) found that students who experienced early retention (grade one) performed between than did those with later retentions (grade eight). They concluded that the assumption that retention will increase the probability of increased subject mastery is specious.

The third type of study, Type III, which compared students having matched educational deficits for which promotion or retention had been experimentally determined, was considered by Jackson to be the most superior. In this design, students who were experiencing difficulties would be identified and randomly assigned social promotion or retention. Then, the two groups' achievement would be inventoried the year following the assignment in efforts to determine significant differences.

Conducting Type III studies in 1983, Phillips and LeDantec arrived at opposite conclusions regarding retention and social promotion. Phillips found that high school students retained in grade eight had better classroom grades then their socially promoted counterparts. Conducting an inquiry similar to that of Phillips on junior high school students, LeDantec examined the mathematical reasoning and reading achievement subtests the year of retention and the year following retention of the students and ound no significant differences between the two groups. Confirming LeDantec's findings was Gilbert's (1984) five-year study on students in grades four through eight in the area of reading achievement. He found little difference existed between the students who sere socially promoted and those who were retained. He argued that his findings suggested that social promotion was no more valuable than retention in improving reading achievement.

Baenen (1986) conducted a five-year longitudinal study on students in grade one who were retained with low achievers who were socially promoted. Examining their reading and mathematics scores on achievement examinations, the retainers exhibited some increase in their achievement examinations, the retainees exhibited

91

some increase in their achievement during the repeated year but regressed thereafter. By the fifth year of the study, the students who had been socially promoted, although low achieving in grade one, showed higher scores than the retained group. Both groups, however, occupied a lower position than did the regularly promoted students in achievement results after the first grade. Consequently, Baenen recommended that placement with special help was a better alternative for most low achievers than retention.

Westmoreland (1993) conducted similar research upon students in grade seven who were advancing to grade eight. The 1704 eighth-grade pupils who were registered in six inner-city middle schools were examined. Of this group, 181 students had been socially promoted and 44 students retained with the remaining 1479 promoted. The students' achievement results on the total mathematics, total reading, and total language subtests of the *Metropolitan Achievement Test* (MAT 6) taken at the conclusion of their eighth-grade school year were examined. On all subtests, the promoted students scored significantly higher than did students in either of the two lower classifications. Similarly, the retained students performed significantly better than their socially promoted counterparts. Westmoreland's empirical results did not support the supposition that retention was a viable option for the academically challenged student, however; when it is compared with social promotion, it is the preferable option.

Reducing Student Failure

Since empirical evidence has indicated that social promotions should be terminated, school districts might consider applying some of the following strategies to reduce the possibility of student failure:

1. Identify and publish specific performance objective criteria to be satisfied at key grades.
2. Identify student academic deficiencies promptly to arrange appropriate instructional remediation strategies.
3. Encourage and emphasize early childhood literacy in the home.
4. Provide high-quality curriculum and instruction to all students.
5. Furnish staff development programs that strengthen teachers' content knowledge while improving instructional strategies dedicated to engaging all students in learning.
6. Publish explicit expectations for both families and the community to reduce confusion regarding promotion.
7. Offer summer school programs for students who fail to

achieve high academic success.

8. Increase instructional time through tutoring, before and/or after school programs, homework hot lines, or year-round schooling.

9. Lower the class size in the primary grades.

10. Allow a teacher to teach the same students for more than one year for consistent instruction.

11. Establish transitional and dropout prevention programs in the secondary schools.

12. Make schools accountable for academic performance by publicizing student performance results and/or intervening in low-achieving schools.

School districts who initiate policies to reduce student failure must realize that they require not only effort but also many resources to effect success. The monetary requirements to provide summer schooling and transitional programs could be astronomical. However, the attitude of achievement generated after successful program completion by the marginal student far outweighs the district's expenditure.

Student Retention Perceptions

While educators are pondering the question of retention or promotion, the perceptions of students regarding the question should be considered. Several researchers have surveyed students regarding the practice of retention. Byrnes and Yamamoto (1985) interviewed seventy-one students who were enrolled in a school district of 26,000 elementary students in a large southwestern border city who had been retained in grades one, three and six while also interviewing the same number of promoted students. They found that the students were reluctant to admit their retention and, thus, used such adjectives as, "bad, sad, upset or embarrassed," (1985, p. 209) to describe their feelings at being retained. Forty-seven percent of the retained students reported that they had received some form of punishment after being retained. The investigators reported that the retained students found it difficult to think of something positive about not being promoted. The teachers of the retained students observed that the parents were more emotional regarding the proposed retentions than were the students.

These empirical findings appear to reinforce the conclusion that retained students perceive themselves to be failures. Believing

95

this, these students often express a distaste for formal education, which manifests itself through discipline referrals.

Demanding Results

Good teachers have specific objectives, or standards, in mind as they design their lessons for their students. The objectives detail what the student is expected to recall, replicate, manipulate, understand, or demonstrate at some in the semester. The teacher will decide how close to the established standard the student has arrived and this will determine the student's promotion or retention.

Many states have adopted standards for what they believe students should know and tests to measure whether young people are learning. They are anticipating that these legislated standards will improve achievement in the classrooms. At present, forty-eight states now test their students with nineteen of them requiring the students to pass a state test to graduate from high school. Six states have laws, which will link student promotion to test results while forty states have standards in all core subjects. Thirty-four states have gone beyond multiple-choice tests to include performance questions in their assessment systems.

These state-mandated minimum competency tests which are admissions to the next grade or graduation from high school have evoked serious questions regarding the testing process:

1. Are the tests valid?

2. Do they have construct and content reliability?

3. Are the tests discriminatory to special populations ?

4. Do the test reflect the information taught in the classroom lessons?

5. Have the competencies being tested been identified thoroughly?

Objections for Minimum Competency Testing

Those who oppose determining the fate of students through minimum competency testing believe:

1. *Tests are culturally biased.* Many of the questions to be answered have a vocabulary and frame of reference which is not native to many cultures. The student, not being exposed to the given vocabulary or experience, will fail to answer the question properly. This will provide a false sense of achievement failure. A white student might have difficulty understanding a question regarding, "playing the

97

dozens," while his black peer might falter on a question about croquet rules.

2. *Tests are economically biased.* Many questions posed on examinations can be answered because the students have had access to reading materials, computers with the Internet, or cultural events. Students from low socio-economic backgrounds have not had the opportunity to read all of the magazines provided in the homes of their more affluent peers. A single- parent of several children does not have the time or money to provide the children with educational opportunities that a nuclear family can offer. Questions designed to test a plethora of different experiences will be hazardous to the economically challenged student.

3. *Tests are not valid nationwide.* There is no standardization of testing criteria throughout the forty-eight states. Some tests choose to emphasize language arts and mathematics while others measure information learned in the core curricula disciplines. So, what is considered as being *competent* in one state does not demonstrate competency in another.

4. *Teachers will teach to the test.* Because the schools are

being held accountable for academic achievement, teachers will begin teaching only the information expected to be tested on the competency test. This will limit the scope of learning by the students and little opportunity will be provided for critical thinking.

5. *Schools will be controlled by the government.* Since the state legislators are mandating the test specifications for the competency examinations, there are concerns that the schools will lose their authority and autonomy.

6. *Tests damage student self-esteem.* Students who do not master the competency requirements, fill face a loss of self-esteem when their successful peers boast about their passing test results. This could result in an increase of student dropouts.

Proponents for Minimum Competency Testing

Advocates for minimum competency testing postulate that:

1. *Tests validate minority discrimination.* Test results indicate that minority students have not have the opportunity to receive a high quality   education and, thus, suffer discrimination when given a standardized competency examination.

2.   *Tests are diagnostic.* Test results allow teachers and students to determine competency objectives which require additional attention.

3.   *Tests document retention.* Test results provide the evidential support for teachers to recommend retention.

4.   *Tests results have no emotional consequences.* Advocates do not believe the test results to be damaging to the students' self-concept.

Financial Deliberations

When implementing a program of competency testing, the school districts must give some consideration to the impact upon the budget. Often, state legislatures mandate programs with little thought to the cost of implementation. An increase in the school district's budget might be seen because of the following:

1.   *Test construction.* It is very expensive to construct a valid and reliable standardized test locally. In addition to designing the test questions, the test must be administered to a pilot group and norms established. After making revisions on the test items, the test must be reprinted to distribution. The majority of states have developed their own standardized tests, however; these have been subjected

100

to numerous lawsuits by angry parents whose children are being retained.

2. *Test administration.* Many states assume the responsibility of designing, distributing, and grading the standardized tests. However, if the school district decided to administer a practice examination, it will have to pay for copies of previously administered examinations and purchase answer documents. Additionally, the district or school campus may have to purchase machines for scoring the answer documents.

3. *Remedial programs.* One of the primary expenses to a school district are the remedial programs, which must be implemented to assist failing student to achieve parity with their successful peers. When creating a program, the cost of paying teacher salaries can be astronomical.

4. *Community Cooperation.* While the cost of securing community cooperation about competency testing and retention may not be expressed in dollars, the effort spent in convincing the public can be very time consuming. Rhetoric regarding retention is quite convincing until it is applied to one's own child.

Parental Participation

It is unrealistic to expect that the school educators can accomplish the task of student learning without the participation of the student's parents or guardians. It is the unique student who will retain all instructional information given during his time spent in the classroom if reinforcement of the instructional skills is not conducted within the home. Among the many strategies which schools have utilized in providing assistance to parents with their children's academic training are:

1. *Training Workshops.* Workshops conducted for parents regarding such topics as nutrition, nurturing, discipline strategies, and study skills will assist the parents in enhancing academic learning.

2. *Resource Centers.* Establishing resource centers within the school with information and tips to help their children in specific curricula areas will draw the parents into the school. For example, having computer laboratory available with software installed for the different subjects to be mastered would allow the parent and child to interact at the school.

3. *Literacy Programs.* In communities having families with

limited English-speaking abilities or minimum educational experience, evening literacy programs would be beneficial.

4. *Home-School Contracts.* A contract, which enumerates the responsibilities of the school, and the home for student achievement is often helpful.

5. *Volunteer Opportunities.* Involving the parents in the school's activities through volunteer opportunities will form a positive bond between the school and the parent for the mutual betterment of the student.

6. *Information Communication.* When the school informs the parents of activities and policies through newsletters and parent meetings, the parents will be more supportive of the school's agenda.

Statistics have demonstrated that there is a positive correlation between the amount of parental involvement in school activities and student achievement. As the parents receive information from the school through some of the above-mentioned strategies, they can partnership with the school in their child's educational success by:

1. *Emphasizing academic excellence.* Parents can reinforce the importance of good study habits and perseverance to achieve academic excellence while in school.

2.   *Monitor academic progress.* Parents can supervise students' homework and review students' progress on their report cards to monitor academic progress. It is very mysterious to administrators, when parental complaints are received regarding a student's failure in a specific course, to be told that the parent has never viewed a report card during the entire semester nor communicated with the student's instructor.

3.   *Encourage reading.* Parents of elementary school children should engage in reading activities with their children at least thirty minutes each night. Secondary school parents should transport their children to the public library and encourage avid reading.

4.   *Attend school events.* When parents attend the open-house events and other teacher conference meetings, their children see evidence of the importance of an education.

Community Commitment

The often quoted African proverb, "It takes an entire village to raise a child," is very true. Schools must solicit the community's support for its programs to be successful. Communities must volunteer their resources to the schools in the quest for academic achievement.

One viable source of community support is within the religious community. Many churches offer tutorial programs for remedial instruction. Religious leaders can urge student scholarship by encouraging students to remain in school acknowledging student success through award recognition ceremonies.

The business community has a vested interest in student achievement because students need to acquire skills for future employment. They can offer monetary incentives and employment opportunities for students who remain in school and are academically successful. Additionally, they can provide tutors and mentors for students during and after school. The businesses could allow students to "shadow" one of their employees to observe the reality of the job's responsibilities. Additionally, they could use some of their budget to finance cultural and academic field trips for the enrichment of the disadvantaged population.

Summary

Sir Richard Livingstone observed wryly, "Theories are more common than achievements in the history of education" (1978, p. 233). Educators have offered divergent opinions regarding appropriate educational prescriptions for the academically ailing at-risk student. The choices for intervention have either been retention or social promotion. The research findings, which have been conducted mainly on elementary aged students, have been viewed or identified as being biased, depending upon the type of design the investigator utilized.

Researchers supporting retention have contended that the practice will allow the at-risk student to achieve a more solid academic foundation, one that will ensure successful completion of schooling. However, these proponents have suggested retention be done in the primary grades to be effective. Retention enthusiasts have also argued that social promotion or grade placement generates feelings of inadequacy in those students who are placed as a result of an inability to compete successfully with their promoted counterparts.

On the other hand, investigators have supplied empirical evidence that retention has not assured the at-risk student subject mastery by virtue of a second exposure to teaching methodologies, which the student initially found incomprehensible. In fact, the at-risk minority students have been the victims of the majority of the retentions placing them in a position of isolation and possible withdrawal from schooling.

The current philosophy is for merit promotion with the benchmark being competency based standardized examinations. As might be expected the competency based testing has its advocates and objectors with each group professing validations for the preferred choice. Since the majority of states now require competency based testing, there are financial considerations, which school districts must review.

Schools must enlist the support of parents and the community to change from the old choices of social promotion or retention to those of retention or merit promotion. Schools should be committed to providing parents with training to assist their children with instruction. Additionally, schools should encourage parental volunteerism to strengthen participation in school activities.

Because there are many factors, which contribute to students' being identified as at-risk for retention, the authors would like to suggest that school personnel adapt a new paradigm addressing their instruction. First, staff development should be conducted to apprise teachers regarding the identification of potential at-risk retainees. Teachers must realize that students cannot dismiss the extraneous influences upon entrance at the classroom door.

Second, teachers must be encouraged to adopt teaching methodologies, which appeal to the divergent learning styles of the class members. The *old lecture method* of the 1800s will not suffice to entice the attention-deficit, video aficionado of the 1990s to achievement.

Thirdly, teachers must understand and implement positive motivational strategies. It is the wise instructor who realizes that students, more often than not, are motivated to learn for the sake of their teacher rather than for the for the subject material being introduced. There is not an administrator in the United States who has not heard from a recalcitrant student the reason for noncompliance or failure was a personality conflict with the teacher.

Fourth, and certainly not the least in importance, the old saying that "all children can learn," should not be lip service from teachers. All children *will learn* if they perceive that the instruction is interesting, relevant, and inspirational. To achieve this goal and reduce the retention statistics for the at-risk student will require much planning and cooperation from administrators, teachers, parents, and the community at large.

References

Ames, L. (1981). *Retention in Grade Can Be a Step Forward.* The Education Digest, 46, 36.

Baenen, N. (1986). *Prospectives After Five Years-Has Grade Retention Passed or Failed?* (ERIC Document Reproduction Service No. 300 424).

Balow, I. And Schwager, M. (1990). *Retention in Grade: Failed Procedure (p. 3).* (ERIC Document Reproduction Service No. 315 710).

Byrnes, D. and Yamamoto, K. (1985). *Academic Retention of Elementary Pupils: An Inside Look,* Education, 106, 209.

Carstens, A. (1985). *Retention and Social Promotion for the Exceptional Child.* School Psychology Review, 14, 55-56.

Ebel, R. (1980). *The Failure of Schools Without Failure..* Phi Delta Kappan, 61, 386.

Gesell, A. (1974). *Infant and Child in the Culture of Today* (p.6). New York: Harper & Row.

Gilbert, S. (1985). *Effects of Retention of Reading Achievement Among Elementary School Students.* (Doctoral dissertation, Purdue University, 1984). Dissertation Abstracts International, 45, 3243A.

Gutierrez, M. (1983). *The Effects of Nonpromotion of First Through Fourth Grade Students as Related to Academic Achievement, Self-Concept and Intellectual Maturity.* (Doctoral

109

dissertation, Northern Arizona University, 1983). <u>Dissertation Abstracts International, 44,</u> 984A.

Harness, C. (1984). *The Ramifications of Grade Retention: An Annotated Bibliography of the Literature* (p. 9). (ERIC Document Reproduction Service No. 225 348).

Hess, F. (1978). *Promotion vs. NonPromotion: A Policy Review.* (ERIC Document Reproduction Service No. 158 398).

Jackson, G. (1975). *The Research Evidence on the Effects of Grade Retention.* <u>Review of Educational Research, 45,</u> 613-665.

Kerzner, R. (1982). *The Effects of Retention on Achievement.* (ERIC Document Reproduction Service No. 216 309).

Labaree, D.F. (1999). *Setting the Standard: The Characteristics & Consequences of Alternative Student Promotional Policies.* (ERIC Document Reproduction Service No. 239 368).

Livingston, R. (1983). In Murphey, E., *Webster's Treasury of Relevant Quotations* (p. 233). New York: Greenwich House.

McAfee, J. (1981). *Towards a Theory of Promotion: Does Retaining Students Really Work?* (p. 7). (ERIC Document Reproduction Service No. 210 871).

McDaid, J. and Baca, C. (1987). *Promotion and Retention Policy Implementation Policy.* (ERIC Document Reproduction Service No. 294 982).

May, D. and Welch, E. (1984). *The Effects of Developmental Placement and Early Retention on Children's Later Scores on Standardized Tests.* Psychology in the Schools, 21, 381.

Miller, M., Frazier, C. & Richey, D. (1980). *Student Non-Promotion and Teacher Attitude.* Contemporary Education, 51, 157.

Oldham, B. (1982). *The Longitudinal Effects of Pupil retention Practices in the First Three Grades.* (Doctoral dissertation, University of Kentucky, 1982). Dissertation Abstracts International, 43, 3772A.

Ozmon, H. and Carver, A. (1990). *Philosophical Foundations of Education (4th ed.).* (p. 212). Columbus: Merrill Publishing.

Peterson, A. (1983). *A Longitudinal Study of the Effects of Retention/Promotion on Academic Achievement.* (ERIC Document Reproduction Service No. 263 667).

Santayana, G. (1986). *The Life of Reason.* In Bhole, B., *The Home Book of American Quotation.* (p. 280). New York: Dodd, Mead & Company, Inc.

Schuyler, N. (1986). *Promotion or Retention- Have Policies Passed or Failed?* (p. 8). (ERIC Document Reproduction Service No. 288 904).

Schwager, M., & Balow, I. (1990). *An Analysis of Retention Policies and Their Possible Effects on Retention Rates.* (p. 12). (ERIC Document Reproduction Service No. 318 572).

Walker, E., & Mahere, S. (1985). *Multiple Retentions: Some Consequences for the Cognitive and Affective Maturation of Minority Elementary Students,* Urban Education, 22, 86.

Walker N. (1984). *Elementary School Grade retention: On Avoiding Abuses Through Systematic Decision-Making.* Journal of Research and Development in Education, 18, 2.

Westmoreland, D. (1993). *An Analysis of Selected Variables Associated With the Promotional Status of Urban Middle School Students.* (Doctoral dissertation, Texas Southern University, 1993). Dissertation Abstracts International, 55, 1900A.

Wright, J. (1981). *The Measured Academic Achievement of Two Groups of First Grade Students Matched Along Five Variables When One Group Has Been Retained.* . (Doctoral dissertation, Temple University, 1979). Dissertation Abstracts International, 41, 3418A.

Yoshida, S. (1989). *A Meta-Analysis of the Effects of Grade Retention on the Achievement of Elementary School Children.* (Doctoral dissertation, Fordham University, 1989). Dissertation Abstracts International, 50, 1213A.

CHAPTER 9

The Uphill Climb To Erase White Racism in America and Its Effects on Urban, School-Aged Children

Sabrina A. Brinson, Ph. D.
The University of Memphis
Memphis, TN

Laws against teaching slaves, black codes, and the infamous case of *Plessy vs. Ferguson* were some of the key factors that solidified segregation in America. The primary reason for segregating African Americans has remained constant. It is white racism, a centuries-old system intentionally designed to exclude Americans of color from full participation in the economy, polity, and society. (Feagin & Vera, 1995, p. 9). Namely, Anglo Americans felt that African Americans were an inferior race, and should only hold subservient roles in society. In the early 1800s, heavy legislation against teaching slaves was implemented. Some thought it would deter the free African Americans from communicating with the ones in slavery, and others reasoned African Americans who could not read would remain unaware of antislavery arguments. "Most blacks lived in slavery in the South, where education was considered a threat to the security of the slave

113

labor system. Masters maintained that 'an educated slave was a dangerous slave'" (Conrad & Shrode, 1987, pp. 35).

Operating out of fear and insecurities that African Americans would unite into formidable forces, Anglo Americans devised methods to block their progress and education. Nevertheless, slavery was eventually abolished and opportunities for African Americans to advance were becoming available, until a notable case for segregation reared its ugly head. In 1896, *Plessy vs. Ferguson* made it legal to segregate Anglo Americans and African Americans on public transportation. Declaring that the separation of races was not unconstitutional was the opening many were looking for to utilize their own rules and laws to keep African Americans away from Anglo Americans in most settings such as schools, busses, restaurants, and religious institutes.

"Separate but equal" accommodations were a facade. Many Anglo Americans rebelled at any type of education for African Americans, let alone an equal one. A number of outrageously biased laws and practices were made possible by the *Plessy vs. Ferguson* decision. African Americans were forced to hold school in shabby buildings, their books were outdated and torn, they had insufficient writing utensils and supplies, and no transportation was provided. As a result, African Americans were forced to walk up to

15 miles to get to school while school buses transported Anglo Americans students to schools only 11/2 miles away. On the national average, approximately $500.00 a year was allotted per African American student, in comparison to approximately $1,400.00 a year per Anglo American student. "Though the promise was 'separate but equal', inequality in financial support prevented African Americans from achieving this equality. The United States Supreme Court even held constitutional a Georgia school segregation law providing state funds for white schools although there were no provisions made for Negro schools." (Stoff, 1967, p. 5).

Turning points in segregated education came in the early 1930s. Federal, state, and local research studies were conducted, comparing Black and White educational programs. The results proved "separate but equal" educational systems were not equal. This revelation gave African Americans ammunition to apply for admission to white graduate schools. When they were denied admission they climbed the legal ladder, from local courts all the way to the Supreme Court when necessary. To illustrate, Donald Murray sued for admission to the University of Maryland Law School and won in 1935. The court ruled that Murray was entitled to attend since Maryland did not have a "separate but equal" law school for African Americans. In 1938, when Lloyd Gaines applied for admission to the University of Missouri Law School, the state offered Gaines a partial scholarship to attend any law school in any state other than his own. The Supreme Court ruled the out-of-state scholarship denied Gaines equal protection of the laws. "...he (Gaines) was entitled to equal protection of the laws, and the state was bound to furnish him within its borders facilities for legal education substantially equal to those which the state (provides), for persons of the white race, whether or not other Negroes sought the same opportunity." (Jackson 1975, p. 80).

Gaines was admitted, but to ensure no other African Americas would be, Missouri built a law school at an established Black college. Other states reacted to these two Supreme Court decisions by rapidly establishing the necessary schools. Additionally, southern states actually began to spend more money on Black secondary schools to give the appearance of two "separate but equal" school systems. However, the dent was indelible, and the mirage began to vanish. In 1950, Herman Sweatt won the right to be admitted to the University of Texas Law School. This was a major victory because Texas had a Black law school, but Sweatt argued it was impossible to obtain an equal education in a law school that was hurriedly set up in the basement of a building. The Supreme Court ruled a Black professional school was not equal to a White one. The "separate but equal" policy had disintegrated at the higher education level!

The most direct and far-reaching victory in the battle against segregated education was achieved in 1954, in the phenomenal case of *Brown vs. the Board of Education of Topeka.* The decision attacked the segregation issue and opposed the previous "separate but equal" doctrine.

> To separate them (children in grade and high schools) from others of similar age and qualifications solely because of their race generates a feeling of inferiority as to their status in the community that may effect their hearts and minds in a way unlikely ever to be undone... We conclude that in the field of public education the doctrine of separate but equal has no place separate educational facilities are inherently unequal. (Stoff, 1967, p. 7).

This ruling by the Supreme Court illuminated an explosive course for desegregation in elementary, middle, and high school settings. Melba Patillo Beals, Elizabeth Eckford, Ernest Green, Gloria Ray Karlmark, Carlotta Walls LaNier, Terrence Roberts Jefferson Thomas, Minnijean Brown Trickey, and Thelma Mothershed Wair integrated Central High School in Little Rock, Arkansas in 1957. Spearheaded by Governor Faubus, who instructed the National Guard to bar them from the school, the

117

resistance to integration was so intense that President Eisenhower had to assign soldiers from the 101st Airborne Division to accompany them to and from classes, and restore order to Little Rock. Even still, these high school students who were known as "The Little Rock Nine" faced angry mobs and endured relentless threats, verbal taunts, and acts of violence on a daily basis for an entire year. In her memoirs, *Warriors Don't Cry,* Melba Patillo Beals reflected on her experience when she said;

> So we headed down a path from which there was no turning back. because when we thought of alternatives, the only option was living our lives behind the fences of segregation and passing on that legacy to our children. Today, when I see how far we have progressed in terms of school integration, in some instances I am pleased. In other areas, I am angry. Why have we not devised a workable plan for solving a problem that has so long plagued this nation? We put a man on the moon because we committed the resources to do so. Today, thirty-six years after the Central High crisis, school integration is still not a reality, and we use children as tender warriors on the battlefield to achieve racial equality (Deals, 1994, p. 310).

Likewise, in 1960, in a flurry of belligerent protests and confrontations six-year-old Ruby Bridges became the first African American student to attend William Frantz Elementary School in New Orleans, Louisiana. Horrendous battles about desegregation have been fought and won in the United States. Yet, philosophies

118

and practices infiltrated with white racism, prejudices, negative stereotypes, and racial preferences still plague America.

It is also important to note that over four decades after the 1954 Supreme Court Ruling for desegregation in schools, African Americans are still accomplishing educational milestones. To illustrate, in 1998, I became the first African American to obtain a doctorate degree in Curriculum and Instruction with an Emphasis in Early Childhood Education, at one of the largest research universities in the United States. While I was "walking through the fire" of the doctoral program, I had to dodge and endure a steady flow of flaming darts. Incidents like a White professor who repeatedly scheduled appointments with me and never showed up, White peers who conveniently forgot to tell me about meetings for group presentations, and an overall lack of invitations from members of the mainstream to engage in scholarly activities that were designed to heighten professional development were just a few. Nevertheless, it was a gratifying and sweet experience. Sweet indeed because of the invaluable knowledge, skills, and expertise that was added to my repertoire. Therefore, in step with my mentoring predecessors, it is my honor and responsibility to pass on the priceless legacy of education. Also, it is my privilege to ensure that little ones on Black Street can dream in color with their eyes wide open.

Definition of Terms

Bias: Any attitude, belief, or feeling that results in, and helps to justify, unfair treatment of an individual because of his or her identity (Derman-Sparks, 1989).

Ethnic Identity: Ethnic identity is one's sense of belonging *to* an ethnic group and the part of one's thinking, perceptions, feelings, and behavior that is *due* to ethnic group membership (Rotheram & Phinney, 1986).

Prejudice: The most salient characteristic of prejudice is its negative. hateful quality. Prejudice is defined by this negativity. More precisely, prejudice refers to an organized predisposition to respond in an unfavorable manner toward people from an ethnic group because of their ethnic affiliation. In addition to making unfavorable or negative judgments, a person must possess two other features if he or she is to be called prejudiced. One is an underlying organized predisposition to feel negatively toward people. Another is that the negativity be directed toward persons because of their ethnic or racial group membership, and not only because of some individual attribute (Aboud, 1988).

120

Race: According to Bahr, Chadwick, and Strauss (1979) race is a term "purely social in origin". Race is defined as an individual's membership in a group based on physical/biological traits and characteristics. Several centuries of scholarly attempts to demonstrate a sound biological basis for race classification have merely served to underscore its inconsistent and transitory nature." (p. 145).

Banks (1991) concurs with the concept of race as a social construct:

> Physical anthropologists attempt to divide the human species into subgroups on the basis of biological traits and characteristics. They use the concept of race to differentiate between the various human subgroups. However, anthropologists have had considerable difficulty in trying to structure valid racial categories because of the wide variety of traits and characteristics that human groups share, the extensive mixture among groups, and because the racial categories they have formulated have been largely arbitrary. Consequently, the schemes they have developed for classifying human races vary greatly in number and in characteristics (p. 73).

Racial Attitudes: Racial attitudes are the beliefs or opinions that an individual has for a particular race. An individual's racial attitudes may be categorized as prejudiced or nonprejudiced.

Racial Preferences: Racial preferences are attitudes in favor of someone or something. To illustrate, an Anglo American preference means that the person exhibits more positive attitudes toward Anglo American people than toward African American people.

White Racism: In the United States, white racism is a centuries-old system intentionally designed to exclude Americans of color from full participation in the economy, polity, and society. (Feagin & Vera, 1995; p. 9).

Numerous theories about prejudice have been developed over the years. The Inner State Theory (Adorno, Frenkel-Brunswick, Levinson, & Sanford; 1950) surmised that prejudice is a reflection of an internal state. The Group-Norm Theory (Sherif & Sherif, 1953) proposed that the formation of prejudiced attitudes is functionally related to becoming a group member. Allport (1954) posited that the group's preferences must become the individuals' preferences, along with the group's enemies becoming his/her enemies. Pate (1994) hypothesized that we do not make a decision to become prejudiced; instead, prejudice is a type of socialization. Individuals form opinions of people in the same manner that we form opinions of our world, our culture, and ourselves. Yet, some people form strong prejudices, while other people are generally free of prejudiced attitudes.

Investigations about racial attitudes and racial preferences began over sixty years ago (Branch & Newcombe, 1986; Clark & Clark, 1940; Plous & Williams, 1995). Results revealed that the development of racial attitudes begins very early in life. Infants notice racial cues and by the age of 3 or 4, most children have a rudimentary concept of race and can accurately apply socially conventional labels of "Black" and "White" to pictures, dolls, and people (Katz, 1976).

According to Allport (1954), children learn to evaluate ethnic groups the way their parents do either by direct training, although it is very rare, or by observing and imitating their parent's verbal and nonverbal behavior. Once children understand what group is referred to a label, their negative emotion becomes crystallized into a negative attitude and total rejection of the group. Later, it becomes integrated with their whole personality; and thereby becomes stabilized and difficult to change. Collectively, information received in home, school, and community settings along with messages disseminated through the mass media signal what is important to individuals. These messages have both short and long-term impacts on an individual's self-worth and productivity.

The uniqueness of the American slavery experience and the challenge of living thereafter as an African American constructed a distinctive folklore. Achieving a sound ethnic identity has become a primary goal for many individuals in the struggle against white racism. Rotheram and Phinney (1986) defined ethnic identity as "one's sense of belonging to an ethnic group and the part of one's thinking, perceptions, feelings, and behavior that is due to ethnic group membership" (p. 13). Also, ethnic identity is important because children as young as three have been found to indicate favorable attitudes towards, and a preference for, Anglo Americans (e.g., Anglo American doll is given in response to the instruction, "Give me the doll that is a nice doll."). These pro-Anglo American attitudes have been found in both Anglo American and African American individuals. Unfortunately, many of the pro-Anglo American attitudes were accompanied by anti-African American attitudes (e.g., African American doll is given in response to the instruction, "Give me the doll that looks bad".). These findings support the notion that cultivating the ethnic identity of African American children may enhance many aspects of their emotional and social adjustment. For example, children who achieve ethnic

124

identity tend to have a higher sense of self-esteem and demonstrate more positive family and peer interactions.

The Anglo American preference that is indicated by children as early as the preschool years may be due in *part* to society's multi-faceted propensity to embrace Anglo Americans. To illustrate, the content and images of children's literature have the power to enhance young children's racial acceptance of their own ethnic groups, as well as others. Unfortunately, the portrayal of African Americans in literature may have inhibited acceptance of African American individuals. Namely, African American characters have changed over time from being notorious to being almost invisible. Before the Civil Rights Movement, a lot of the books published for children exploited the African American experience. Vividly animated picture books like *Billy Whiskers in the South, Little Black Sambo, The Inky Boys, The Pickaninny Twins* and Wooden White were disseminated by widespread demand, and held in high regard by readers.

> Prior to the Civil Rights Movement, standard portrayals of African Americans in children's literature were not particularly positive. Typically depicted was a "no count natural thief, a flunky happily steppin' and fetchin', a pitied simpleton, a gargantuan bully and, (ever popular) a poor, helpless, inept underdog scared senseless, a shakin' and a quakin' in his shoes, many of whom rattled off unintelligible dialect." Accentuating the text were

125

characters illustrated in charcoal black with out-of-control hair and absurdly over-exaggerated features that seemed to leap off the pages (Brinson, 1997, pp. 8-9).

The impact of books which thoroughly distorted experiences also had the probability of psychologically damaging children. Consequently, a tidal wave of literature of this nature helped spark the Civil Rights Movement. After which, the African American image was ameliorated in literature. However, the quantity of children's books that depicted characters with African heritage was severally underrepresented. Larrick (1965) conducted a study of 5,200 books published from 1962-1964, which revealed that only 347 (6.7%) of them included an African American character in the text or illustration. Furthermore, only 47 (0.9%) of the books examined had African Americans that were represented in contemporary settings. In the mid-1980s, only 1% of children literature was about African Americans (Bishop, 1987). More recently, over 5000 children's books were published in 1990. However, only 51 of these were written and/or illustrated by African Americans. That figure amounts to less than 2% of all children's books. (Cooperative Children's Book Center, 1991). During that same year, only one children's book written by an African American was a best-seller (Robacks, 1991). That book was *Roll of Thunder, Hear My Cry* (Taylor, 1976).

126

If literature is a mirror that reflects human life, then all children who read or are read to need to see themselves reflected as part of humanity. If they are not, or if their reflections are distorted and ridiculous. there is the danger that they will absorb negative messages about themselves and people like them. Those who see only themselves or who are exposed to errors and misrepresentations are miseducated into a false sense of superiority, and the harm is doubly done (Harris, 1992, p. 43).

To date, the preferences of African American children may have been swayed toward Anglo American individuals partly because they are heralded in most of the current literature for children, as well as dated classics that omitted racial groups in their entirety or were racially assaultive. Currently, there still remains a critical shortage of culturally conscious books portraying the African American experience with cognizant characters and suitable vernacular. Also, notably missing is an adequate number of African American authors and illustrators who undoubtedly have the expertise and inside track desired to create stimulating stories set in African American homes and communities, adorned with kaleidoscopic illustrations that depict the accurate variations of African American people.

Contributing to Anglo American preferences may also be the myriad of toys, dolls, and action figures overwhelmingly representative of Anglo Americans. They are highlighted publicly and readily available to children. Moreover in the majority of cases when companies do manufacture African American versions, they are identical to the Anglo American ones except for skin color. Hence most of the African American dolls and action figures are not representative of the true variations of skin color, hair, and features of individuals of African descent.

Society's preference for Anglo Americans is also demonstrated through the preferential treatment these individuals receive. To illustrate, television programs and movies primarily feature Anglo Americans in notable roles for which many of them receive various honors. In contrast, accolades for the achievements of African American thespians are few and far between. Hattie McDaniel was the first African American to receive an Academy Award for acting in a supporting role in 1939. That award was not shared by another African American until 43 years later when Louis Gosset, Jr. received it for best supporting actor in 1982. Furthermore, Sidney Poitier received an Academy Award for best actor in 1962. To date, he is still the only African American to receive an Academy Award for best actor.

Additionally, a significant part of our self-worth is shaped by how others view and react to us. African American individuals receive poignant messages from infancy through adulthood that they are not valued as much as their Anglo American peers. For instance, African Americans were required to get permission to vote under the United States Constitution. In 1965, the Voting Rights Act had to be created to give African Americans that right to vote- a right that is granted at birth for Anglo American individuals in the United States. More insulting still to African Americans is the insinuation that they are not just different, but deficient. Overall preferences for Anglo Americans are rooted in the very fabric of our country and reinforced by daily distinctions of privilege for these individuals. Consequently, the lack of such privileges for African American children lay the foundation for them to indicate preferences for Anglo American individuals, sometimes at the expense of forsaking their own uniqueness.

To counterbalance off-kilter Anglo American preferences, parents and teacher educators should continue to design and implement interventions that will foster more positive acceptance of African Americans and other ethnically diverse groups. The works of Banks (1988, 1991) stress the importance of race in education to facilitate favorable attitudes and to counteract the negative attitudes expressed by children about their own as well as other racial groups. Hence all children should be involved in daily classroom curricula that integrates knowledge about outstanding achievements of African Americans like the following; Patricia E. Bath, a physician who invented the Cataract Laserphacoprobe, which is a medical instrument to remove cataract from the eye; Harmon L. Grime, the inventor of the Folding Wing Aircraft, which was used in combat on aircraft carriers; Mae C. Jemison, a physician who became the first African American woman astronaut in the world, and she traveled into space on Space Lab; and Elijah McCoy who is known as the Father of Lubrications because he automated the lubrication process of the railroad engine with a device called the drip cup and procured more than 56 patents for improved versions of it, along with inventing the Steam Cylinder Lubricator, lawn sprinkler, and ironing table (Robinson, 1999).

Active participation in the uphill battle against the white racism that continues in the 21st Century requires students to be aware of how prevalently it is practiced across numerous situations. For example, in 1989, Carol DiMaiti, a White expectant mother was shot in the bead while driving with her husband through the Mission Hill area of Boston, Massachusetts. Her injured husband, Charles Stuart, said that he and his wife had been shot by a Black man. The Boston police responded quickly. More than one hundred police officers stopped numerous Black men in the area in an attempt to find the murderer. The ruse became clear when Stuart's story eventually unraveled. Subsequently the mass media spotlighted the ruse, a television movie retold the story in 1990, and the next year Joe Sharkey published a book, *Deadly Greed*, detailing the story of Carol Stuart's murder.

> The cover of the book reads: "What would make a young husband kill his pregnant wife? DEADLY AMBITION. What would make him think he could blame a black man for the crime? DEADLY ARROGANCE. What would make the police and media believe his story and shake a city to its core? DEADLY RACISM (Feagin & Vera 1995, p. 64).

"We Want to Change" was the title of a proposal devised in Dubuque, Iowa in 1991. The purpose of the plan was to recruit Black families to enrich the diversity of the city's population. The reaction? Some of the White citizens engaged in racial attacks on Black residents that included cross burnings, hate messages and physical harassment. In addition to the smoking crosses and racist vandalism, hate letters and racist graffiti were directed at local Black residents and White supporters of the recruitment plan. The dozen Black students at the overwhelmingly White Dubuque Senior High School (which had 1,471 White students) were racially harassed and police officers patrolled the halls to deter violence. The Dubuque case illustrated that white racism including violent acts can happen anywhere in American even in a

131

predominantly White, midwestern city that has no history of plantation slavery or extensive legal segregation (Feagin & Vera, 1995, p. 19).

Texaco paid the largest racial discrimination law suit settlement in history in the amount of $176.1 million, after the release of tape recordings in which Texaco officials used racial slurs to describe Black employees (Tatum, 1997. p. 193). Moreover, African American employees and job applicants filed a class-action job discrimination law suit against Shoney's one of the largest family restaurant chains in America in 1989.

> The suit charged that Shoney's had turned away black applicants and relegated the few it hired to kitchen chores. Black employees stated that they were assigned the least desirable hours. Even some white supervisions reported that they were fired or threatened with demotion if they refused to obey instructions to restrict black employment in the company A former assistant manager reported that she was told to darken the "O" in the Shoney's logo on job application forms to indicate that an applicant was black (Feagin & Vera, 1995, pp 47-48).

A class-action law suit was also initiated against the Denny's family restaurant chain by a group of African American government arenas. They reported that they waited for almost an hour when fifteen Anglo American agents and customers who

132

entered the restaurant after they did were served quickly and repeatedly.

> On April 1, 1993, Dan Rather opened the CBS evening news with a statement about black secret Service agents. As a Flagstar executive remembered it, Rather said, "They put their lives on the line every day, but they can't get served at Denny's." (Feagin & Vera, 1995, p. 56).

In conclusion, there are many individuals who charge that the racism snake has been beat dead. Not! A simple glance at America's tapestry shows that it is still alive, writhing with venom, and on constant strike, all too often with lethal injections.

> There have been race riots in Los Angeles and St. Petersburg, Florida. A thirteen-year-old black boy was beaten into a coma by White youths who caught him riding his bicycle in their Chicago neighborhood. Anti-immigrant legislation in California has led to the public harassment of Latino citizens. Anti-Asian violence has increased dramatically (Tatum, 1997, p. 193).

When incidents like these vanish from America's biased actions, when all tall, dark, and handsome men can successfully hail taxis; and when the vehement chants of "Two, four, six, eight, we ain't gonna integrate!" have faded from the collective mind, heart, and soul of the United States, multiethnic integration will be a tangible reality. Until then, *The Story of Ruby Bridges* reminds us that *Warriors Don't Cry,* when faced with adversity in the uphill climb to ease *White Racism* in America.

Books Cited

Bannerman, H. (1945). *Little Black Sambo.* New York: Harrison.

Beals, P. (1994). Warriors Don't Cry. New York: Washington Square Press.

Cole, P. (1995). The Story of Ruby Bridges. New York. Scholastic.

Gruelle, J. (1927). Wooden Willie. Chicago: Donahue Publishers.

Feagin, J. R., & Vera, H. (1995). White racism. New York: Routledge.

Hoffman, H. (1876). Inky Bovs. New York: McLoughlin Bros.

Montgomery, F. T. (1917). Billy Whiskers in the south. New York: Saalfield.

Perkins, L. F. (1931). The Pickininny Twins. Boston: Houghton Mifflin.

Sharkey, J. (1991). Deadly greed: The riveting true story of the Stuart murder case that rocked Boston and shocked the Nation. New York: Prentice Hall.

Taylor. M. (1975). Roll of thunder, hear my cry. New York: Dial.

References

Aboud, F. E. (1988). Children and prejudice. New York: Basil Blackwell.

Adorno, T. X., Frenkel-Brunswick, E., Levinson, D. J. & Sanford, R. N. (1950). The authoritarian personality. New York: Harper and Row.

Allport, G. W. (1954). The nature of prejudice. Cambridge, MA: Addison-Wesley.

Bahr, H., Chadwick, B., & Strauss, J. (1979). American ethnicity. Lexington, MA: D. C. Heath and Company.

Banks, J. A. (1988). Multiethnic education (2nd ed.). Boston: Allyn & Bacon.

Banks, J. A. (1991). Teaching strategies for ethnic studies. Boston: Allyn and Bacon.

Banks, J. A. (1991). Teaching multicultural literacy to teachers. Teaching Education, 4, 35-144

Beals, M. P. (1994). Warriors don't cry. New York: Washington Square Press

Bishop, R. S. (1987). Extending multicultural understanding through children's books. In B. Cullinan (Ed.), Children's literature in the reading program, 60-67. Newark, DE: International Reading Association

Branch, C. W., & Newcombe, N. (1995). Racial attitude development among young Black children as a function of parental attitudes: A longitudinal and cross-sectional study. Child Development, 57, 712-21.

Brinson, S, A, (1997). Literature of a dream: Portrayal of African American characters before and after the Civil Rights Movement. Dragon Lode, 15(3), 7-10.

Clark, K. B., & Clark, M. K. (1940). Skin color as a factor in racial identification of Negro preschool children. Journal of Social Psychology, 2(15), 169.

Conrad, C. F., & Shrode, P. E. (1987). The long road: Desegregating higher education. The National Educational Association Higher Education Journal, 35, 34-44.

Cooperative Children's Book Center. (April 5-6, 1991), The multicultural mirror: Cultural substance in literature for children and young adults. Madison, WI: Annual meeting of the Cooperative Children's Book Center.

Derman-Sparks, L (1989). Anti-bias curriculum: Tools for empowering young children. Washington, D. C.: National Association for the Education of Young Children.

Feagin, J. R.., & Vera, H. (1995). White racism. New York. Routledge.

Harris, V. J. (1992). (Ed.). Teaching multicultural literature in grades K-8. Norwood, MA: Christopher-Gordon Publishers.

Katz, P. A. (1976). Towards the elimination of racism. New York: Pergamon.

Jackson, F. (1975). The Black man in America: 1932-1954. New York. Franklin Watts.

Larrick, N. (1965, September). The all-white world of children's book. The Saturday Review, 48, 63-65.

Pate, G. S. (1994). Defenses against prejudice. The High School Journal, 78(1), 60-65.

Plous, S., &. Williams, T. (1995). Racial stereotypes from the days of American slavery: A continuing legacy. Journal of Applied Social Psychology, 25(9), 798-817.

Robacks, D. (1991, March). Commercial books scored big with kids. Publishers Weekly, 238, 30-35.

Robinson, V. J. (1999). Little known black history facts. Volume one. Oak Brook, IL: McDonald's Corporation.

Rotheram, M. J., & Phinney, J. S. (Eds.). Children's ethnic socialization: Pluralism and development. Newbury Park, CA: Sage.

Sherif, M. & Sherif, C. W. (1953). Groups in harmony and tension. New York: Harper.

Stoff, S. (1967). The two-way street guideposts to peaceful school desegregation. Indianapolis: David-Stewart Publishing.

Tatum, B. D. (1997). <u>Why are all the black kids sitting together in the cafeteria?</u> New York: Basic Books.

CHAPTER 10

Multicultural Education In Urban Schools

Dr. Darlington I. Ndubuike
Houston, TX

<u>Introduction</u>

In my years of teaching, I have come to the conclusion that every teacher in the classroom does his or her best in an attempt to impact knowledge to the students. Although we may not all succeed in this attempt, there is always that urge and burning desire to make instruction effective. Because a teacher's success is ideally measured by the success of his/her students, it becomes unquestionably important that much energy be channeled and expended toward designing and implementing effective instruction, which necessitates learning and achievement of every student. For students to achieve, teachers must achieve. It is my desire in this chapter to motivate teachers in multicultural classrooms to soar above their fears and personal doubts and taste the sweet, fresh air of professional satisfaction. It is my desire to get them to know that they are free to break and push boundaries in their creative

141

exploration and not limit themselves within the confines of the text and patchy curriculum inherent in departmentalization.

Departmentalization is an excellent concept. It allows teachers the opportunity to focus on the subject areas of their strength, which, in turn benefits the students who are the recipients of this knowledge. Most of the time, however, teachers in a departmentalized setting tend to do their own things. Students leave a science classroom to a social studies classroom without any link whatsoever from one subject area to the other. This fragmentation of instruction due to departmentalization and incoherent sequencing in curriculum results in disjointed and disintegrated accumulation of information, which, in turn, results in the inapplicability of the information, acquired.

The purpose of this chapter is to provide teachers with effective strategies for instructional design in a multicultural, multi-linguistic multiethnic, and multi-ability classroom which avails opportunities for cohesive learning and for making cross-curricula and multi-cultural connection. My main objectives are: (1) To present a process of multicultural instructional design; (2) To demonstrate the use of multi-cultural, cross-cultural, multi- and cross-disciplinary instructional strategies using cultural phenomena; (3) To identify strategies for exploring a central

142

theme, phenomenon, or experience and making cross-cultural and interdisciplinary connections; and (4) To experience anthropological exploration and identification of cultural artifacts and paraphernalia.

The strategies presented here (1) require students to draw on principles and skills associated with more than one discipline, (2) generate developmentally appropriate activities, (3) increase student performance, (4) provide opportunity for life-long learning, (5) encourage cooperation and collaboration within grade levels, across grade levels, and among teachers, and (6) provide entry points and opportunities for success for learners with diverse learning styles, varying ability levels, and cultural experiences.

Teachers will take a "trip" to the culture in question and, using the *Travel Agency Model,* conduct research and provide specific information relating to this culture. They will engage in experiences specific to cross-curricula instructional strategies in the different subject areas.

In this presentation, I have used art as a nodal point---a point where all the elements of instruction, learning, and culture seem to intertwine. My experiences as an all-level art teacher over the years in the United States, added to my years of experience as a classroom teacher in another country, have taught me that effective

143

instructional design and effective instructional delivery must make use of the resources which art has to offer. As Hamblen (1986) notes, every culture produces and responds to art in one way or another. Besides, art is every child's second nature and it represents, without doubt, every culture's most distinctive product. Therefore, it has a very important part to play in a multicultural classroom. It is the most expedient way to tap into the interest of the children and gain access into the recesses of their inner being. It makes diversity possible without a shock, communicates across language and cultural barriers, and reaches that which is fundamental in human nature. Its images and sound speak to, move, and touch people of all ages, diverse learning styles, varying ability levels, backgrounds and cultural experiences (Hamblin, 1986).

Art is that silent part of the child that is in constant communication with the unseen, with nature, and with the world beyond, revealing the unspeakable mystery of human nature. When children are creatively engaged in their work; they conjure silence, the original stillness that permeated the universe in the beginning-before and during creation. It is that same silence that permeates the children's world as they are engaged in creative activity, putting them in constant communion with the unknown voices of the

144

imagination, the spirits that wield the brushes, the pencils, the pastels, and the pens with the Creator's precision. The whole idea of this presentation is to enrich teachers' multicultural instructional repertoire, trigger their creative nerves, and awaken that creativity in them.

Cultivating a healthy school culture: The Multicultural Implications

The crux of multicultural education is the understanding of the inner reality of the students---their belief systems, their state of mind, and the way they interpret the world. Teachers must endeavor to find out what the ontological values of each student are, and in what ritualistic ways the student attempts to understand the world and the functions of such rituals (Sergiovanni and Starratt, 1993). The problem of the teacher in a multicultural classroom is more than simply translating a language; "it is one of human understanding" (Courtney, 1980, p. 25). It is a serious error for teachers to assume that all students have the same learning styles or the same style traits as the group taken as a whole. After all, argues Guild (1994), "effective educational decisions and practices must emanate from an understanding of the ways that individuals learn, and knowing each student, especially his or her

145

culture, is essential preparation for facilitating, structuring, and validating successful learning for all students" (p. 16).

In other words, teachers in multicultural classrooms must endeavor to understand their students and tap, at regular intervals, into their students' cultures, to know what their students know, their personalities and characters, their moods and self-concepts, their flexibility and biases and how best to relate to them. Teachers should show concern for the students in their classrooms who are lost because they have not been culturally mainstreamed, and are therefore dormant and missing the opportunity of being educated. They must not allow their own values and preferences to interfere with reaching out to those students in their classrooms whose cultures are different from theirs. For effective teaching to occur, the teacher must know his/her students and respect their diverse cultural backgrounds.

Problem in the multicultural classroom

The problem in the multicultural classroom is that teachers who are culturally deficient attempt to teach children who are culturally different (Gay, 1986). This cultural deficiency and lack of confidence on the part of teachers stem from lack of knowledge of minority and non- Western cultures and the failure to include a

146

comprehensive multicultural education curriculum in teacher professional preparatory programs. Many teacher preparatory programs do not provide teachers with the what, when, where, who, and how of the information they need in order to be effective as multicultural educators (Tomhave, 1992). Teacher education preparatory programs should be structured such that they equip teachers with the knowledge and understanding they need to effect change in the ways that they teach in the multicultural classroom. Baptiste (1994) indicates that "American schools have become mono-cultural environments that present only a narrow view of the essence of human experience through the western civilization curriculum" (p. 93). To make the plight of ill-prepared teachers worse, multicultural experiences that are available for in-service teacher training are inadequate and, worst still, optional, making teachers very reluctant to change the routine they are accustomed to.

Converting the natives

Tomhave (1992) emphasizes that the only way one could understand a culture foreign to him or her is by immersing oneself into that culture. However, the teacher does not need to take the students to Africa in order for them to experience African art,

147

although that would be wonderful. It is important to note that effective teaching and learning of any culture cannot be done in isolation. The teacher must endeavor to create an environment suitable for that experience to occur.

Consider this:

Doe Elementary School is a small inner city school located in the southeast side of Houston. It is a predominantly minority elementary school in a low-income area. The current enrollment at Doe averages between 470 - 480 students. The school's ethnic population stands at 97% Black (which includes students from Africa and the Caribbean) and 3% Hispanic. Approximately 97% of the students are enrolled in a government-subsidized program. The average attendance rate is 94% with a student mobility rate of 44%. Although the present population of the school includes only 3% Hispanic, the percentage is growing.

Five years ago, the school's population was 100% African-American. It becomes important that the school begins to acknowledge and accept the presence of this and other cultures.

During one of the talent shows at school, parents were invited. The cafeteria was full of parents who came to see their children perform. One of the families in the audience was from

Mexico, and they had just moved to Houston and enrolled their three children at Doe. One of the children, the oldest daughter, Melissa, was performing. She was very proud to have made it successfully through the rigorous audition and selection process. So, her entire family was present to see her performing and to cheer her on.

When it came time for her to do her song, the "Labamba, " she took the center stage. Everyone was quiet. Suddenly, a loud scream cracked through the air and ripped the silence. It sounded like the crowing of a rooster. Everyone turned to the direction of the scream. It was Melissa's father. He was cheering his daughter on.

When Melissa and her siblings arrived at school the following day, the students began to flap their "wings" and make the "rooster" sound in front of them. Melissa didn't find it funny. It kept her and her siblings miserable. Melissa must have told her parents. Her father came to the school to complain to the principal. It was then that he explained the reason for the scream in. If only the students knew' that the "rooster" scream was an affirmation of performance in Mexico.

Cultivating a cohesive and healthy school culture requires creating a supportive environment that is conducive to student learning and teacher growth. It calls for the establishment of a climate that is nurturing for all subcultures within the school, a climate in which every culture represented in the school is recognized, understood, and, as much as possible, acknowledged and accepted. It really does not matter if the school is 100% Black, 100% White, 100% Hispanic, or 100% Oriental; the students still need to be exposed to the various cultures of the world. The fact of the matter is that sometime, somewhere in their lives, these students will have to interact with people from other cultures either at work or at play. No one knows where people's future careers or life's endeavors will lead them. Acquaintance with a variety of cultural values and styles will enrich the educational experience of all students and help prepare them for life in a multicultural society (Smith, 1980, p. 82).

The need for cultural awareness schools is urgent. Literature abounds in multicultural education that recognizes the importance of preparing educational leaders and teachers for culturally diverse schools and classrooms. For multicultural education to succeed, principals and teachers must embrace a multicultural approach to education and provide both the

150

environment and the instruction conducive to the goals of multiculturalism. Institutions must prepare future teachers and administrators to address not only the educational needs of their students, but their cultural needs also (Baptiste, 1999). Schools must be restructured to meet the needs of this ethnic, linguistic, and cultural diversity (Banks, 1997). It is essential that the curriculum reflect the culturally diverse nation so that everyone can gain appreciation of the diversity that exists (Baptiste, 1994).

Staff development programs must be in place for those teachers currently working in schools to provide them with information about the various multicultural teaching strategies and learning styles. Teachers must be aware that they are faced with the task of creating a multi-cultural environment to suit the potpourri of cultures in their schools. Today, more than ever, this need has become even more pressing now that the United States is experiencing a huge multicultural influx and substantial change in ethnicity (Banks, 1997); now that most schools in America serve a culturally diverse student body (Manning and Baruth, 1991).

As people from different parts of the world come to America for different unique reasons, they bring their unique individual cultures and differences. Their children bring to the classroom life experiences that are unique and different from

151

everyone else's due to a unique and valuable cultural heritage. Concerned teachers must be aware of the growing complexity of this ethnic mix.

The complexity has become even more convoluted as all ethnic groups strive to retain their cultural heritage and ethnic identities. Teachers must therefore sense this urgency and develop approaches, instructional strategies that are more comprehensive and more holistic and allow for truly global viewing of the world, and especially those of the many different cultural groups represented in their schools, approaches that would include not only the recognition, acceptance, and support of all cultures, but also a gut-level respect for human differences. This, therefore, calls for a more stringent look into the educational programs and activities designed to accommodate this multi-ethnic, multi-cultural, multi- linguistic upsurge in the classrooms.

It calls for the restructuring of educational priorities, commitments, and processes to reflect the reality of this multi-pluralistic phenomenon that is a fact of life in the United States; a commitment to achieving unity in diversity. It calls for teachers who are adequately prepared and ready to do whatever it takes for the interest of all the children.

A good, multicultural teacher is not one who has traveled all over the world. It is not a teacher who speaks all the different languages of the world. It is a teacher who is dedicated, a teacher who is competent and motivated, and a teacher who can and who will. It is one who sees in the eyes of every child the desire to succeed and excel, regardless of cultural background and individual differences.

Multicultural education concerns itself with the relationship between cultures, between student and teacher, between school and society. It concerns itself with not only the understanding of cultural differences, but most importantly, with the positive endorsement of such differences (Banks, 1997). It creates opportunity for the recognition of similarities that exist among and between individuals and groups, the plurality of the ethnic and cultural backgrounds of these individuals and the acceptance of such plurality, because, as Best (1986) notes, "the identity of a human being and the character of his thoughts and feelings cannot intelligibly be regarded as independent of his culture" (p. 34).

There is more to multicultural education than curriculum content (Banks, 1994). Multicultural education includes teaching for equitable student achievement and acting to reduce prejudice. Study shows that students perform poorly in school when they are

153

discriminated against by their teachers (Reek, Reck and Keefe, 1993). The failure to try to understand the different criteria of other societies creates a tendency to depreciate them (Best, 1986).

Art in multicultural education

Reinforcing the artistic heritage of all cultures can help build a positive ethnic self-image. Every culture produces and responds to art in one way or another (Hamblen, 1986). Therefore, any strong and realistic multicultural curriculum should incorporate the study of multi-cultural, cross-cultural, and historic art forms.

Art transcends not only academic and literary boundaries but ethnic and cultural boundaries as well; it bridges the gap between cultures, promotes the transmission of cultural heritage (Boughton, 1986), speaks universal language (Hamblen, 1986), and reaches that which is fundamental in human nature. Its images and sound speak to, move, and touch people of all backgrounds and cultures (Grigsby, 1989). It is a strong means of achieving unity in the world and enhancing cross-cultural understanding of similarities and differences. It is this understanding and appreciation of differences that create bonds between people (Grigsby, 1986).

154

Art instills a sense of integrity and dignity in the children of all cultures and renews cultural identity and pride from generation to generation (Feldman, 1976). It makes explicit the concepts of reality, the meaning of the universe, and the interpretation of the cycles of human life (McFee, 1980). When properly introduced, art could provide opportunities for students to gain knowledge of the art from other cultures by understanding the context in which the art was created and the function of the work of art in that society. This understanding, laying the groundwork, could help them extend this learning to their own cultures and discover, through art, that culture is not a hermetically sealed unit. They will see behind the cloud of cultural diversity that there are common interests.

When art exemplars from diverse ethnic groups are included in instruction, it will not only benefit the mainstream culture, but also serve to bolster ethnic pride and reinforce collective cultural identity among the minority group (DiBlasio and Park, 1983). However, when art exemplars from ethnic minority groups are not included in instruction, it "provokes a negative reaction from those of similar cultural or ethnic backgrounds. It is like looking in the mirror and seeing no reflection. Just as the artist doesn't exist, the students of the same ilk become non-persons" (Grigsby, 1986; p. 19). When the cultures of minority children are

155

recognized, it improves their chances for academic success and lead to more tolerant attitudes among children of the majority culture.

Teaching the art of a non-Western culture requires more than simply passing on knowledge acquired overnight from textbooks or magazine articles. To effectively teach the tribal art of Africa, for example, the teacher must, among other things, acquaint him or herself as much as possible, with the roles of tribal arts in African cultures and the social and cultural history of the people who originally made and used the art (Clark, 1990).

The creative teacher

The creative teacher is a multicultural teacher; one who is equally as multiculturalized as his/her classroom; a teacher who is acquainted with a variety of cultural values and styles, which will enrich the educational experience of all the students and help prepare them for life in a multicultural universe.

A creative teacher is like a good physician; (s)he not only makes the right diagnosis, but (s)he also writes the correct prescription for a cure. However, one thing sets the creative teacher apart. In addition to making the right diagnosis and writing the correct prescription for a cure, the creative teacher also personally administers it. (S)he is knowledgeable about and sensitive to students' differing cultural backgrounds, values, and traditions. (S)he provides a classroom atmosphere in which students' cultures are recognized, shared, and respected, develops culturally appropriate curricula materials that supplement those whose treatment of differing cultural groups is limited, and gives students an opportunity to explore what they do not know or understand about other cultures.

A creative teacher is a quality teacher. A creative teacher understands the different learning styles and inner realities of his/her students and leads them onward into a learning that is natural to them. In a race to the finish line contested by a dog and a snail, it is quite obvious that the dog will outrun the snail and embrace the ropes first, but the snail will eventually get there. It requires extra effort on the part of the snail and encouragement on the part of the coach. It requires teachers who involve students in examining universal human systems and weighing cultural influences, teachers who show concern for the students in their classroom who are lost because they have not been culturally mainstreamed and are therefore dormant and missing the opportunity of being educated. These students are like crabs on a dry land, which need just a sprinkle of natural water to come to life again. Water, which is a part of the crab's natural habitat, is a revitalizer, a resuscitator; hence a little tapping into a student's culture will bring the dormant, unresponsive student back to life in the classroom.

A creative teacher does not settle with an old worn out adage: "You can lead a horse to the stream, but you cannot make him drink." A creative teacher takes the horse to the stream and makes the horse drink. In fact, (s)he does not need to "make" the horse drink; the horse becomes thirsty and looks forward to getting to the stream due to thirst. Like a radio evangelist once said, "You must add salt to the horse's oath, so, by the time the horse reaches the stream, he is ready to drink, and drink copiously!". It requires effective planning and designing. A little hype and enthusiasm would help. A creative teacher must start ahead of time to motivate the students and point them toward the lesson ahead. It must be a lesson that begins from where the students are, a lesson that is designed with the children's *"backpack"* in mind. Such lessons are replete with fun learning activities that are designed to touch and reach every child.

Creative teachers do not allow their own values and preferences to interfere with reaching out to those students in their classrooms whose cultures are different from theirs. They know their students and respect their diverse cultural backgrounds.

The teacher as furniture maker

A creative teacher is a multicultural teacher. Therefore, as a teacher in a multicultural classroom, you are expected to, and must teach, every child assigned to you regardless of the contents of their individual *"backpacks"*---the extent of their differences. Unless you understand the child, you will have difficulty adapting instructional methods to the needs of the students. It is the individual differences of the students---their culture, learning styles, and experiences---that drive your instructional design, the contents of your lesson and your instructional delivery.

A multicultural teacher is like a furniture maker who fashions the most beautiful pieces of fine furniture from different kinds of wood. Most of the wood (s)he receives come from different forests, in different colors, shapes, and forms. Some of the wood (s)he uses come to him/her in raw logs; others come half-broken, with missing parts, and others come processed and ready to assemble. Regardless of the situation and origin of the wood, his/her task is the same---to make beautiful furniture suitable for the market. However, one thing is sure---whether the logs make it to the market depends on the ability and skill of the furniture maker, his/her patience and courage, his/her persistence and tenacity, but most importantly, his/her understanding of the different types of wood and the direction of their grains. It is the failure to chisel with the grain that causes the wood to chip.

A creative teacher therefore pays attention to individual differences, because no matter from which forest the wood comes, it is the responsibility of the furniture maker to fashion it into fine furniture suitable for the market. Understanding individual differences among learners helps the teacher to adapt instructional methods to the needs of the learner (Bunch, 2000).

The teacher as gardener

Every year, before and during planting season, the gardeners get to work. They till the ground ready to plant the seed. They go to the garden shop and research to find the best combination of fertilizer to use for their soil, knowing that if they bought the wrong one, it could kill their seeds even before they grow. They, therefore, spend time and expend energy in this process. In the garden, they empty the combination on to the soil and mix. Then they water and nurture. As soon as the soil is ready,

160

they plant their seeds. They watch the seeds sprout and grow into beautiful tendrils.

Then come the weeds. The gardener must detect and uproot the weeds around the little plant. Bad weeds around the plant obstruct the healthy growth of the plant. Soon, it becomes difficult to separate the weeds from the good plant.

Then comes the rain. The little tendrils could not stand the pressure. They bend in the rain. The gardener patiently and carefully picks up the fallen tendril, adds more soil to its base and attaches a stick to hold it up. This is significant. It is the patience of the gardener, her skill and knowledge of the plant that has saved the little plant from dying, from drying up in the sun, and from being cast away into the garbage. Consider, however, that if the gardener leaves the little tendril unattended, it will stay bent and grow up crooked. There's nothing anyone can do to straighten it now. It becomes a tree whose branches obstruct the road, a "menace to society," and the only way to get rid of this tree is to cut it down and put it away from society.

Teachers as Ethnographer

Most teachers live in a totally different neighborhood than their students and have not been in their students' homes or neighborhoods (Gollnick and Chinn, 1998). They do not know what their students know, and they do not know how to best relate to them. To know and understand their students, teachers must become cultural ethnographers. They must attempt to immerse themselves into their students' cultural systems. Ethnography allows the teachers the opportunity to view holistically the relationships between and within their students' cultures and to interact face to face with their student' families and environments. It provides teachers the opportunity to learn from their students and to see the world from their students' eyes. Spradley (1979) states:

"Ethnography offers all of us the chance to step outside our narrow cultural backgrounds, to set aside our socially inherited ethnocentrism, if only for a brief period, and to apprehend the world from the viewpoint of other human beings who live by different meaning systems" (p. v.)

By eating the food they eat, participating in their ceremonies and rituals, listening to their type of music, talking their talk, and walking their walk; the teacher is in a position to define, interpret, express, describe, and analyze cultural similarities and differences.

The "Backpack" concept

The problem of the teacher in a multicultural classroom is more than translating a language; "it is one of human understanding" (Courtney, 1980, p. 25). It is an error for teachers to assume that all students are alike and have the same learning styles or the same style traits as the group taken as a whole. Effective educational decisions and practices must emanate from an understanding of the ways that individuals learn (Guild, 1994), because the way humans learn is culturally determined.

The crux of multicultural education is in the understanding of the inner reality of the students---their belief systems, their state of mind, and the way they interpret the world. Every student carries a backpack, but the content of the individual backpacks vary. Like the backpacks, each student stores and carries along a unique background, cultural and life experiences, learning styles, and interest. So, what is in your students' backpacks, or should I say background? It is the duty of the multicultural teacher to find out what the contents of their students' backpacks are, the ontological values of each student, in what ritualistic ways the student attempts to understand the world, and the functions of such rituals.

Teachers could "research" their students' backpacks by questioning them about their cultural practices, by engaging them in conversations about their topics of interest. They could conduct research on the different ethnic groups that make up the classroom and the school and engage parents in discussions concerning their cultural practices and preferences (Ogbu, 1992).

You know your students better than anybody else does. You have looked into their backpacks, and you have known what their interests, experiences, learning styles, and ability levels are, and their view of life. The writers of the textbooks do not know these things. They don't have the personal knowledge and information you have about your students. You must therefore use your textbook as guide. In fact, your book is called *The Teacher's Guide,* and you must use it as such. It is there to guide you. Pull the information you need to meet your students needs and tailor instruction to fit in your students' "backpacks." Always look beyond the texts.

Creative teachers understand their students and tap, at regular intervals, into their students' cultures to know what their students know, their personalities and characteristics, their moods and self-concepts, their flexibility and biases, and how best to relate to them. It is the knowledge of each student, especially his or her culture, background, and life experiences that constitute the essential preparation for facilitating, structuring, and validating successful learning for all students (Guild, 1994). Knowing and understanding the cultures of the students. their interests and background, provide the teacher with the opportunity to tailor instruction to meet the needs of the students and make the content more meaningful to them (Gollnick and Chinn, 1998).

A look into each student's backpack reveals that no two students are alike. Siblings carry different unique items in their backpacks. Most of the time, the contents of these backpacks are influenced by some unexplainable innate tendencies that create unique individual experiences; hence even identical twins tend to behave and react differently to the same situations, one haptically and the other visually.

Four types of students exist, and every student falls into one of these four categories:

1)   *The Cannie De Willie:* This represents those students in your class who are dedicated to their work. You know and they know that they can do their work, and they, indeed, do their work. You do not need to stay over their shoulders to get them to do their work. They are motivated. As the furniture maker, these could be the type of wood that comes to you already processed and ready to assemble. They get along well with other students, respect other students' differences, and appreciate their similarities. They are willing to give up some of their own so that others may have. These students can succeed, and they will.

165

2)   The Cannie De Wontie: Like the Cannie De Willies, this category of students possess the ability to perform, but, unlike the Cannie De Willie, they refuse to do so. These are the students who refuse to complete their work in class and at home. You, as a teacher, know that these students have the ability to do the work. You know that they can get along well with other students, but they refuse to do so. As a furniture maker, these could represent the type of wood that comes to you half-broken. These students can. but they won't. You must identify their grains and chisel with the grain. Motivation is the key concept here.

3)   The Cantie De Willie: These students are very delicately imbalanced. They struggle with their work, and are frustrated because they cannot get it right. These students could represent the type of wood that comes to the teacher raw. With a little patience and understanding, the students will realize that they, too, can. Patience and determination are the key concepts here.

4)   The Cantie de Wontie: These students are nothing like the first three. They cannot do the work, and they are unwilling to even try. You as the teacher know that these students would do well if only they could try. They are those who can't and who won't. They could be the wood that comes with some parts missing. Your duty as a furniture maker is to identify the missing parts.   Diligently,

166

the teacher and the student can work together to find the missing parts or create matching alternatives. Again, it takes patience, skill, determination and effective planning.

Planning for instruction : The role of the multicultural teacher

Remember that as a furniture maker, your task is to create a beautiful piece of furniture suitable for the market. As a multicultural teacher, you must teach all the students that come to you, regardless of their situation. Your role is that of a motivator. As a creative teacher, you must get your horse ready before you take him to the stream. You must get your students ready to learn. You must arouse your students' interest and curiosity in the lesson by relating it to their interest, their life experiences, and to things that are of personal relevance to them. It is like adding salt to the horse's oat. By the time the horse gets to the stream, he is ready to drink. What if the horse doesn't want to eat his oats, you ask? Notice that I have not chosen to feed the horse with hare or any other type of food the horse eats. I have specified oats, perhaps because a horse doesn't refuse (Find the type of "food' your students love to eat---the dish they will not refuse.) If you are preparing to teach a unit on the Igbo of West Africa, begin in advance to prepare your students to take a trip to West Africa, to

167

Igboland, where drums speak in esoteric tones, and the masquerades emanate from the land of the dead. Again, find out the contents of your students' backpacks and know what their interests are. Begin to create the environment for this new experience to occur and explain your objectives to them in simple, everyday language.

As a multicultural teacher, you must be the facilitator of the learning experience, applying different instructional strategies and providing the needed prerequisite knowledge necessary for the new experience to occur. You must understand that students attend to the instruction more when their own cultural experiences are included in the lesson. When instructional materials reflect students' cultural background, students feel desired and appreciated, and they see themselves as an integral part of the school community (Gollnick and Chinn, 1998).

Instruction ABC

It is with the above understanding in mind that I have developed the *Instruction ABC Model,* a model for effective teaching practices for the creative multicultural teacher. This model understands, and does not take for granted, the fact that every child (yes, even siblings) has different learning styles, different experiences, different backgrounds, different thoughts about life, and sees things differently. They carry different backpacks with different contents. This model is created on the premise that there are as many ways of learning as there are learners, and that individuals, like the contents of their backpacks. vary. Some backpacks may look alike on the outside, but the contents on the inside are different and serve different purposes. I watch with memorable delight as girls in my class carry their purses religiously to class, to recess, to the restroom, and to the cafeteria for lunch. The contents of their purses are personal and important to them, and they do not want to part with them. An effective instruction must therefore build on students' backgrounds, their life experiences, and their cultural upbringing. This concept has been described earlier as the "backpack" which contains the students' background, experience, and culture (BEC). Effective planning allows the teacher to make decisions regarding instructional procedures, instructional resources and materials, directions, and approaches.

A is the ATTENTION: Effective planning and design constitute a thorough search into the student's backpack. Planning provides adequate opportunity for the teacher to determine what salt to add to the horse's oats, so that when the horse gets to the stream, he is thirsty enough to want to drink. As a creative teacher, you must get your students ready to learn. Whet their appetites and promise to give them the food they love to eat. A student's mindset for a lesson increases understanding (Hunter, 1979). Once you have determined the contents of your students' backpacks--their interests, background, life experiences, prior learning, their current skills, and condition under which successful learning has occurred in the past--- then you are ready to design appropriate instruction for that meets those needs. You choose activities that tap into the students' interest, trigger motivation, and capture mental readiness and the preparedness to learn. knowing, as Barab and Linda (1997) indicate, that knowledge is not separated from the context in which it is used. The learning makes sense because it is applicable to the child's real life experiences and daily life encounters. It is not information that is gathered for use in the future. Having looked into your students' backpacks, you therefore know the different cultures that make up your classroom. Tap into these cultures and make relevant cross-cultural connections as you teach. When a student's culture is mentioned or used in a lesson, the student is likely to feel important. (S)he attends more, participates more. and learns more. On the other hand, when other cultures are mentioned

170

and a student's culture is not mentioned, the student is likely to feel isolated. It is like looking into the mirror and seeing no reflection.

B is the BODY: A well-planned lesson sets the stage for academic learning time. It is a prerequisite to effective instruction and learning. A creative multicultural teacher is like a good physician; (s)he not only makes the right diagnosis, but (s)he also writes the correct prescription for a cure. However, what sets the creative teacher apart is that (s)he not only diagnoses the problem and writes the correct prescription for it, but (s)he also personally administers it. Your knowledge of your children's interests and needs drive your instructional strategies. and aid you in the selection of teaching strategies that will compensate for differences in learning styles and cultural backgrounds. These may include games, simulations, group discussions, field experiences, and visual representations. Creative teachers make their objectives clear. You must state your objectives in behavioral terms, write them clearly and explain them in simple everyday language. Clearly written objectives focus both the teacher and the student. You may post your objectives on the wall or where the students can see them. When the objective is clear, it helps you and your students stay focused, and it also provides a sense of direction. When the objective is clear to the teacher, (s)he makes sure that the

171

instructional resources and the activities which (s)he uses during the less(in align with the objective. Irrelevant materials can be distracting. As I mentioned earlier, if a child understands the rationale for a lesson, (s)he is most likely to attend to the instruction. You must be sure that there is a connection between the present lesson and the previous lesson. For example, you may ask students to review the main ideas from the previous lesson. You then explain the objectives for the day and how they are related to the previous learning. If students learned how to multiply 35 by 2 in the previous math lesson, today they will learn how to multiply two digit numbers by two digit numbers. The students now know that they are going to be working on multiplication. They are focused completely. They know that they are not doing division or addition or subtraction. They know that they are not going to repeat the previous learning. They know that they are doing something related to but different from what they learned yesterday. If students read several essays in the previous. English lesson, in this lesson, they will write their own essays. It is an effective instructional strategy to determine in advance the purpose for a lesson. Does it interest the child? What use is it in the child's real world? Rationale can be exhortative or extrinsic. When students understand why instruction is relevant to their own needs, interests and concerns, they are likely to master the objective(s). Always relate the value of the subject matter to the particular needs and interests of the students. For instance, since students in third grade are beginning to socialize, I suggest that rather than teaching them how to write so that they can write better cover letters for job application, teach them how to write so that they can write good friendship letters to their friends in the class or in another class. Again, you know the contents of their "backpacks" and what their needs and interests are. I do not want to bore you with trying to explain Instructional Input, which includes lecture, presentation, demonstration, modeling, labeling, monitoring, re-teaching, guided practice, and independent practice. However, I do want to point out that in every lesson, for effective instruction to occur, and for learning to take place, each of these aspects of instructional delivery must be visited and revisited. In addition, a creative teacher does not assume the known. You must always start from the beginning and make your way up. Such strategy provides the needed prerequisite knowledge, information, skill, and behavior that allow all students to benefit from the planned instruction. Make sure that the instructional resources you are using, including the questions and the activities that the students are engaged in are aligned with your objective. This will maximize the academic

173

learning time---the amount of allocated time the learner is engaged at a high rate of success.

Demonstration, presentation, modeling, and labeling play a very important role during instruction in a multicultural classroom. Personally, I demonstrate every word and every action when talking and more so when teaching. Because English is not my primary spoken language, I got used to making lots of gestures and body movements, and they work quite effectively. Words like prancing, cavorting and even pouring would present excellent opportunity for gesture. Rather than tell it. show it. If you are reading to your students about making a gingerbread man, make motion of the water being poured into the container. If the character in a story you are reading was prancing or cavorting across the room, prance or cavort (Briggs, 1991). Students learn better when they become a part of the lesson being taught, either by simulating a story or playing a character in a story; and when they can picture the event being described in their 'mind's eye.' My primary four teacher once told the class: *"If you can 't remember what 1 said, remember what I did, because once you remember what I did, you will remember what I said.*

I watched with delight as a first grade teacher read a story to her class about a peddler who sold caps. This teacher became the peddler, carrying caps on her head and walking down the street. She got tired and sat under a tree to rest. The monkeys that were on the tree took her caps one after the other. The story unfolded so beautifully with such thrill, suspension, and drama that the students, including myself, were all watching and listening with rapt interest and fascination. Since we knew that we had the students where we wanted them, the story soon became a math lesson. The students were to figure out how many caps the peddler had left after each monkey took one. The students also figured out how much the peddler would have made if he sold all the caps, and so on. Then the students drew pictures of their favorite parts of the story as an illustration. In Social Studies, the students discussed what they would like to be when they grew up. Then they discussed the different occupations and trade. Their homework assignment was to complete a research on the occupation of their choice. In Science, the class examined the behavior pattern of monkeys and compared it with those of humans. The students smoothly sailed from one subject area to another without having to put away one book for another. His or her interest level was maintained all through, and every student had a chance to participate in the fun-filled activity. This is creativity.

Another first grade teacher did the same with *Johnny Apple Seed.* She started by having the students read the story silently on their own. She then read the story aloud to the students. She had the students act out some parts of the story. They designed a cover picture for the story with a new title, and explained why they had chosen that title. She then lead a discussion on where apples grow, who grows them, and where they could be bought. Then the students drew a bowl of apples as still-life They even cut open the apples, tasted them, and planted the seeds. Finally, she set up a grocery store in the class, and students traded places as store clerks and customers.

You, as a creative, multicultural teacher could do the same thing at all grade levels. Ladson-Billings uses *Cinderella* as an example. In *Cinderella*, for instance, you could explore different cross-cultural concepts. You could examine the concept of beauty, magic, monarchy, stepmother, music and dance across cultures. You could read different versions of the Cinderella story from Africa, China, and other parts of the world.

In discussing the study of ethnic cultures from an interdisciplinary perspective, Banks (1997) presents a vivid illustration of how a concept such as culture can be viewed from the perspectives of a number of discipline areas. For example, by discussing cultural similarities and differences in Social Studies, students are given the opportunity to view the world from another person's point of view. By discussing the role of art in other cultures, one learns more about those cultures and appreciates them more, and so on.

Booker T. Washington once described a teacher who worked for an hour with children, trying to impress upon them the meaning of the words lake, island, and peninsula, when a brook close by would have afforded the children an opportunity to pull off their shoes and stockings and wade through the water. Apart from the thrill of wading in the water, the children would learn more about lakes, peninsulas, and islands in less time than they could have in an hour. Let's assume there was no brook close by. Create one. Take the students out to the playground with a bucket of water. Have them construct lakes and islands and peninsulas.

I am an artist, and I love to draw things on the chalkboard to get my point across. But you do not have to be an artist to draw on the board. I use pictures and actual objects. Although I can make the motion of pouring to show students what I mean, how much better would it be if I actually pour something from one container to another (Briggs, 1991).

Find a way for your students to garner information. Information can be fugitive if not organized for ready retrieval. Every teacher must attempt to get his or her students to acquire knowledge at the mastery level---a level of comfort reminiscent to driving a ear. Initial learning may cause sweaty palms and nervous wrecks, but with time, patience, determination, courage and focus, driving soon becomes something one does without actually paying attention to it. You can drive from one destination to another without being overly conscious of it. The same should be of learning. The ultimate goal should be to bring learning to the fluidity level---a level where content is fairly easily learned.

Demonstrate, Model and Label.

As you present your lesson to the students, show them what you are talking about, talk through and share your thought process. Being told how to do something does not guarantee that the students will be able to do it. If Coach Broadnax tells a student how to pass the ball to another player, it is doubtful that the student could do it, using the correct form without first having Coach Broadnax show, illustrate, or model the correct behavior. It is important that the visual input of modeling be accompanied by the verbal input of labeling. The chefs and artists on Channel 8

178

(Houston Public Television) do a good job of modeling and labeling. You may want to watch them sometimes. For instance, if the lesson's objective states that students will identify in a painting five elements of art, then, in the instructional input, the teacher will name, define, and give examples of five or more elements used by artist to create a painting. The teacher will show a painting where these elements were used and lead a class discussion of that painting, using one of the models for art criticism. If the objective requires students to make butter. using ingredients provided by the teacher, then in the modeling behavior, the teacher uses the verbal input of labeling the steps in preparing the ingredients for making butter while simultaneously modeling *(demonstrating)* the steps. What would your instructional input be if you were to work with an objective that states: *The students will identify the difference between an island, a lake, and a peninsula?*

Provide ample opportunity for students to practice the new learning with your supervision. Take the time to monitor and inspect your students' work, checking their learning status and providing continuous feedback and re-teaching as necessary. If you send a recorded voice to your students, there are no cues to help the students focus or learn. Your voice will continue to play whether the students are listening and understanding or not

179

(Briggs, 1991). The difference between listening to a recorded lecture or teaching a lesson for a television audience and a classroom full of students is that in a television or recorded voice situation, there is no method for the teacher to find out if the students are learning what is being presented in a lesson. In a classroom situation, the teacher has the opportunity to stop at intervals and monitor to check for understanding. You should not go to new learning until you are certain that your students have learned the information presented. As you give students the opportunity to practice on their own, independently, keep in mind the fast learners and the slow learners, and provide them equal opportunity to achieve.

In the race to the finish-line between a dog and a snail discussed earlier, we sometimes find ourselves providing a fun activity for the dog to enjoy while waiting for the snail to arrive. For instance, we create a music center and ask the dog to listen to or play some music while waiting for the snail to arrive. The snail would like to enjoy the music center too, but (s)he never gets a chance to. By the time (s)he arrives, it would be time to start another whole-class activity. The snail becomes frustrated and angry. A creative teacher would apply different instructional strategies. (S)he may ask the dog to assist the snail to the finish-

180

line so that both of them would have time to enjoy the music center before the next activity begins. As the dog teaches or assists the snail, both benefit. Students learn even more when they teach others, and children learn better from each other. Always have a closure for each lesson or each segment of a lesson. To not have any type of closure for a lesson presents the type of error found in written English---the "run-on lines" and the "comma splices." Therefore, always use "commas", "semicolons", "colons", or "periods" as necessary to close each lesson. As you close your lesson, be sure to make the learning outcome practical for the children, something that is relevant to their lives and daily experiences, because when students can relate instruction in the classroom with their daily life experiences, more learning occurs. Leave them with skills that they can readily use on their way to school, in their neighborhoods, at home, at the grocery store, etc.

Multi-cultural and cross-disciplinary teaching approach

Single subject teaching creates a learning vacuum between subjects. When students leave one subject to another, there needs to be a connection made from the previous subject to the other. A creative, quality lesson is the lesson that draws from previous lesson(s), connects to a future lesson(s), and integrates to other subject areas and cultures. I call this approach the "Multi-Faceted Teaching Approach".

Other Subject Areas and/or cultures

This approach to teaching is a multidisciplinary, multicultural, cross-disciplinary, and cross-cultural approach to teaching, which weaves together all the fabrics of academic pedagogy. From the *backpack,* you have determined each learner's interest and prior learning experiences, current skills and understanding, and the conditions under which successful learning has taken place. This background should help you in the design and selection of your instructional strategies.

FROM THEORY TO PRACTICE:

Making Instruction cross-cultural and cross-disciplinary

Many teachers are frustrated and struggle with how to make a regular classroom lesson multicultural. However, they don't need to be. Making a lesson multicultural takes motivation, interest, and creativity. It requires adequate planning.

The Multicultural Festival Model

182

In fact, when one asks teachers how involved they are with multicultural education in their schools, the usual response will be the recounting of the different foods and costumes they have eaten and worn, the different dances they have performed and parades that have taken place during Martin Luther King's birthday, Cinco-de-Mayo, St. Patrick's Day, Kwanzaa celebration, and so on. Celebration of heroes and holidays must be built into the year-round multicultural curriculum. In most schools, teachers and students do not think about these multicultural concepts. As soon as these celebratory moments are over, multicultural education is. It conveys the idea that diversity issues come into play only during celebratory moments with foods, dance, songs, art and crafts, fun, and festivals (Ladson-Billings 1994). He calls this the Multicultural Festival Model.

In this model teachers, students, and parents typically spend lots of time and energy preparing for an all-school activity. Students may do background research about a culture, prepare maps, and help create indigenous costumes. Parents may help to prepare various ethnic foods. On the day of the festival, members of the school community go from class to class, visiting the various cultures, sampling the foods and enjoying dances, songs, and arts and crafts. At the end of the day, everyone agrees that the annual

183

event has been a great success. Then, teachers and students go back to their real work (Ladson-Billings, 1994, p. 23).

Ladson-Billings attempts here to emphasize that multicultural education is not a separate, isolated, once-a-year activity. She contends that the regular year-round curriculum should include a range of cultural perspectives built into instructional content.

There's absolutely nothing wrong with sampling food, listening to music from other cultures, enjoying the dance, art, crafts, and costumes of different cultures. A creative multicultural teacher could do more with these. It could become an opportunity to talk about food taboos and types of food eaten by people from different cultures. Some types of foods are permitted in one culture, but not allowed in another, perhaps due to religious or cultural beliefs. In some cultures, dogs are used as pets and referred to as "man's best friend." In other cultures, dogs are eaten as meat. It may begin to sound disgusting, but think of some cultures where cow meat is forbidden, while in other cultures, it is an everyday menu item. Frog legs could be found in some cultures' menu, but a mere mention of frog may cause someone from another culture to vomit.

Some food taboos are instituted for religious reasons. There are some cultures whose religion forbids members from eating pork, duck, shellfish or eating special kinds of food on special religious observances, such as during Passover and Lent.

Some cultures place great importance on certain foods during certain cultural celebrations. During Kwanzaa, for instance, corn must be a part of the meal. During Thanksgiving, turkey is expected to be served. During New Yam festivals, yams must be eaten, and so on.

In some cultures, food is used as a symbol of unity and oneness, an important family ritual. In Igbo culture, for instance, families eat from one dish. This is a symbol of trust and oneness. In America, families come home for dinner, and this is a time to discuss the activities of the day and share ideas. It is a time for parents and children to interact with one another after a busy day. In some churches, the congregation breaks bread' together as an act of communion (Dresser, 1994), a ritual practiced by many Christians as a sign of commitment and rededication.

Certain foods from other cultures have been adopted by other cultures. In America, for instance, Mexican, Chinese, and Italian foods are popular servings. Although there may be people from other cultures who have been assimilated and acculturated, most people would eat the popular food of the dominant group outside the home, but would prefer to eat their ethnic diet at home. An Igbo person, for instance, would eat hamburger and other ethnic foods, but would not go to bed at any given night without eating *foo-foo*.

Table manners differ from culture to culture. In Igbo, fingers are mostly used to eat foo-foo. The Chinese use chopsticks, while forks and spoons are used by Americans. However, not all foods are eaten with fingers, chopsticks and forks. For example, some foods in America are "finger foods."

Building on interest

Find where the button is and push it. You know the content of your students' backpacks and the right salt to add to their oats. I wrote the following story for a school newsletter, which I published monthly. This story appeared on the front page of the newsletter in place of the principal's monthly message. The students always looked forward to reading the information on the front page of the newsletter, so I quickly used this story in a staff-development presentation to illustrate the concept of Multi-Faceted Teaching Approach. I actually taught this lesson to a third grade class.

...I want to share with you my experience during the Spring break. There were many things that I had planned to do during this break, but sitting down and watching an army of ants parade my front yard wasn't one of them.

One little ant was taking a walk across my front porch when it ran into a dead grasshopper. It circled around this "giant" as if to make sure that it was indeed dead. Certain that it was dead, the little lone ant ran back into the grass and disappeared. Soon, it returned with three other ants that came, as it seemed, to confirm their brother's story. Before long, an army of ants flooded my front porch. What fascinated me was the fearlessness of the ants, their determination, their courage, and, above all, their spirit of cooperation and togetherness. I watched with rapt interest as each ant gave it's all, and, as one ant gets tired, it gives way and another takes its place ungrudgingly. Before I knew it, the grasshopper was in the anthill.

What is there to be learned from these ants? No matter how huge the burden, no matter how high the goal, together, cooperatively, anything is possible. In the land of the ants, a grasshopper is a giant, a huge mountain, yet, the ants were not intimidated.   Each one of us has a special function. We have been blessed individually with different talents, and each one of these talents enhances the other. Together, we can equally move mountains. Together, we can make our lives better and our jobs easier.   It takes commitment; it takes cooperation; it takes courage; it takes collegiality, and above all, it takes love and mutual understanding. I know we, too, can!

THE LESSON

FIRST of all, I had the class read the ant story silently. Then I read the story aloud to the class.

I lead a whole group discussion on the story.

Then I had the students summarize the story in their own words.

NEXT, I divided the class in small heterogeneous groups and had the groups brainstorm the lesson(s) learned from the story. Some examples from the groups include:

Cooperation

Friendship

Togetherness

Same goal

Sharing

Unity

Hard work

Selflessness (Whenever an ant finds food, it runs back
to get others).

I pointed out that hard work always pays off. Regardless of your size, if you work hard and do the best of whatever you are doing, you will be recognized. No matter how little you are or think you are or people think you are, you can achieve any goal that you put your mind to. Ants are so tenacious, relentless, and hardworking that, despite their size, they had a place in the Bible.

Four things on earth are small, yet they are extremely wise: Ants are creatures of little strength, yet they store up their food in the summer (Proverbs 30 : 24-25)

"Go to the ant, you sluggard; consider its ways and be wise! It has no commander, no overseer or ruler, yet it stores its provisions in summer and gathers its food at harvest. (Proverbs 6 : 6 8)

THEN, I had the groups discuss the parts in the story. One of the groups acted the story out pantomimically.
The other group added words to it and acted it out.

NEXT, I had the students illustrate an appropriate cover for this storybook. Then, they generated as many 'ant words" as they possibly could.

Some of the "ant words" they generated include: Antibiotic, Antarctica, Pageant Radiant Plant Immigrant, Brilliant Merchant Atlanta, Gallant, Antler Anthill Cantaloupe, Antique, Antidote, Can't, Gigantic, Fantasy, Fantastic, Anticipate, Anthropology, and Giant.

THEN, I had each group choose one of the words from their list and create a picture from it. If the students chose a word that they did not know the meaning of, they used the dictionary to find the meaning. For example: Using the word *Immigrant,* one of the groups created an art of a person with pieces of luggage descending from an airplane. Another group used an ant as their subject and made a picture of an ant with luggage. I encouraged the students to be as creative as they wanted to be, pushing and breaking boundaries. I had them write a story about this immigrant. Using the word *Pageant,* one of the groups created an artwork depicting a pageant with an ant as Miss America. They named their Miss America and wrote her biography. One of the groups illustrated the word *giant* with a collage of a huge ant. Another group came up with a beautiful collage of a plant to illustrate the word *plant.*

190

THEN, I had the class reassemble as a whole group and had each group present its "Ant Word" pictures to the class. The word was kept secret until the other groups had attempted to come up with the illustrated word.

THE STUDENTS DISPLAYED THEIR WORKS ON A BULLETIN BOARD.

Finally, I had the students illustrate an appropriate cover for the story, and, since the story didn't have a title, the students created titles for the story.

SPELLING PRACTICE

Choose any of the "ant words" on your list and make words from it. Example, anthill? Tan, Hall, Ill, An, Ant, Hill, Till, At, Hat, Lit, Tall, Thin, Hit, All, Hail, Nail, Tin.

From the word, immigrant, the students' examples include

Ant, Grant, Migrant, Rat, Ran, Man, Tan, Grin, Am, Man, Mint, Train, Ran, Rag, Ram, Rain, Grain, Tar, Tag, Trim, Trimming.

Simulation of Native Environment

Creative teachers must attempt to transform their classrooms and school into a multicultural universe. Such an example was a presentation by teachers in Connecticut. The teachers created, as much as possible, an environment that paints a picture of the culture they were studying. I call this approach a "Simulation of Native Environment".

Walking past the open door of the room, visitors could hear the beat of drums and the chanting of voices from a distant place--- unfamiliar perhaps, but strangely exciting. Later, they might walk by the music room and hear the youngsters' own voices singing out in a foreign tongue, clapping to unusual rhythms. Upon investigation, our visitors would discover that we were involved in an intercultural study, bringing a bit of Africa into our country Connecticut classrooms. An African unit in the sixth-grade social studies program places emphasis more on modern Africa than its tribal past. However, the music teacher, Mrs. Anyan, and I decided to bring to the students some of the flavor of Africa's cultural history in order to broaden and enrich their experience.

Mrs. Anyan wore to class a headscarf and wrap-around cloth given to her by friends from Ghana. She taught the students a Zambian song in the Bemba language and a Liberian song in English. They learned to listen deeply to the rhythms in the music while clapping, stomping, swaying, and using our own Carl Orff instruments. In the room the display area was covered with photos of African masks and one original mask loaned by a friend. Discussions centered on tribal ritual uses of the masks, their

192

colors, and materials. I was able to demonstrate some dance movements used in that most lively and important art for, and I made a musical tape from records representing various parts of Africa for use during art activities. Our first project was making stylized figures in dance poses, painted in earth-tone designs. The tape was played as students worked, bringing to the art room something of the atmosphere and rhythms of Africa. Symmetrical figures were cut out on folded paper, and then an arm or leg could be cut and repositioned to make the figure "dance". They were then glued to a contrasting background. Next, sixth graders created their own masks. For a base, they used a box of any kind, altering the shape by adding cardboard. Facial features, particularly noses, were built up and then the entire mask was given several layers of papier-mache strips. The painted features and facial designs brought each mask to life and determined its special character. Students mixed tempera paints to achieve various earth colors in light and dark tones. After painting, they used seeds, beans, ropes, yarns, and assorted bits of improvised materials to enhance their creations. A final project was to create textiles using linoleum blocks. Of course, in Africa, there is a wide range of different sorts of textiles, some very colorful. In ours, we limited the colors to earthly neutrals, and the designs to simple

193

geometric patterns, suggested by the layers of rhythms heard in the music. To grasp the concept of an all-over pattern, students made crayon rubbings of one or two small cut-paper designs repeated on a large piece of newsprint.

They experimented with various ways the designs could be placed to achieve the most interesting arrangements. After this experience, they were able to visualize appropriate designs for linoleum blocks. Blocks were then designed and cut. For cloth, we used donated white sheets, dyed to earth colors, and cut to size. Students chose black, brown, white or orange printing inks. For variety, some combined their block with another by someone else in printing their textiles. After the cloth was printed and dry, it was hemmed. When the textiles, masks, and figures were finished, and the African songs and rhythms learned, we felt we had opened the eyes and ears of those young Americans to a beginning understanding of another culture, one not that far away (Farris, 1985, pp. 34-36).

Universal Masking Phenomenon

This strategy is based on the truth that cultures are not sealed units. Mask making, for instance, is a universal phenomenon. The teacher could stimulate the interests of all the students from various cultures by recognizing the universality of masks. Further than that, (s)he could solicit students to name various uses of masks in their different cultures and the different materials used. This will give every student the opportunity to share different cultural values and realize in the process that culture is not a hermetically sealed unit.

In teaching art, the teacher needs, as Stuhr, et al. (1992) emphasized, "to consider and recognize the contributions that each culture makes to other cultural groups (p. 18). Students could be asked to find similarities in function, in motif and in materials used, comparing, contrasting and discovering cultural influences. Katter (1991) encourages teachers to "involve students in examining universal systems, weighing cultural influences, and testing personal criteria and standards of excellence" (p. 28).

I have chosen the mask of the Igbo of West Africa as my focus for this strategy since I lived in that culture and am familiar with the art and culture. To present this lesson, the teacher could begin with the masks worn in America. Most people have worn masks at one time or another for fun. Have the children give examples of times when they have worn masks or seen masks. A good example for the students would be Halloween. The teacher

195

could begin by conducting a brief discussion about the origin of Halloween:

Halloween has its roots in the ancient New Year's Festivals and Festivals of the Dead. In the 19th Century, the Christian church set aside November 1 to honor all its saints, and this date became known as All Hallow's or All Saints' Day. The mass that was said on this day was called Allhallowmas. The evening before this day was referred to as All Hallow's Eve, or All Hallowe'en, and eventually Halloween (Borten, 1965). In anticipation of the evil spirits, people would come to this ritual dressed in costumes made of animal hides and masks made of animal heads; they would light their sticks to take back to their homes to light their hearths. Present day Halloween masks are no longer limited to animal heads; people make up all kinds of masks to represent all kinds of things and people.

Explain that other cultures and countries make masks and wear masks but for different reasons. Discuss uses of mask by firefighters---to protect them from harm. Other people wear masks for festivals, religious rituals, and theatrical presentations, healing and for various reasons.

Explain that in Igbo, people make and wear masks to protect them from harm and for other reasons, such as masquerade

196

dancing, and to act the role of a spirit or ancestor. Then give a brief general function of mask carving in Igbo:

- Portrays belief in ancestral power and the existence of spirits.

- Provides a means of communicating with the dead fathers of the clan through whom they receive protection, power and fertility---they are evoked during harvest to give them thanks, during sowing to ensure fecundity and good harvest, for rain in time of drought, for peace in time of dispute.

- The essence of mask carving is the establishment of relationships with the supernatural powers---the visible expression of the invisible.

- Acts as a temporary dwelling place for a god or spirit.

- Furnishes the means by which the pressing problems of existence can be comprehended and resolved.

- If one is threatened by demons or evil spirits against whom he cannot do anything with his/her natural resources, the person solicits the active intervention of the good spirits by way of sacrifice and invocation.

- Embodies the gods of fertility; women desiring children tie masks on their backs; young girls are given masks to ensure fertility.

- Absorbs the life force that escapes from a human being or from an animal at the moment of death. Entraps the power of other worldly spirits whose dangerous wandering must be protected.

- Used whenever evil spirits are shown to have caused harm to the community.

- Represents dead ancestors whose arrival among the living is announced by the sound of bells and horns.

- Used to fight against any evil spirit that will interfere with any activities of the whole society before the day of ceremonial performances.

- Serves executive agents.

Discuss the carver and the carving process, the materials used. Point out that other cultures around the United States make masks the same way and for the same reason the Igbo do, for religious purposes---to tap vital energy, to honor ancestors, to reflect their ways of life.

Discuss the mask of the Native North Americans. Like the Igbo, they create their mask with wood. They also make masks to reflect their ways of life and their religious beliefs. Like the Igbo their masks are closely tied to nature. They also make their masks to honor their ancestors. In both cultures, it is the men who personify the particular masks, and the mask dancers lose their personal identity to take on the spirit they evoke.

Other cultures that make and use masks like the Igbo include the Eskimo who use masks for festivals, religious ceremonies and initiation. The Eskimo mask, decorated with animal motifs, the animals that the wearer of the mask wishes to become, is believed to capture the spirit of the animal represented by the mask. Whereas Igbo mask is used to drive away the spirit of the dead, the Eskimo mask is used to summon the spirit of animals. However, both masks share some common elements---they serve as guardians to the wearer and are made with the same material-- wood. Other cultures also use wood to make their masks, for example, the Seneca masks, the masks of the Iroquois Indian tribe of North America, the Japanese masks, the American Indian masks, the Mexican masks of the Mayan culture, the masks of the Hopi tribes of Native Americans.

The Teotihucan funeral masks, like the *Agbogbo Mmuo* mask of the Igbo, are used for funerals. All the cultures mentioned above make masks for similar purposes---for funerals, religious purposes, festivals, and rituals.

Explain that many cultures believe in spirits and think that when a person looks like someone or something else, it is easier to communicate to spirits that resemble the one who is communicating. The Eskimo Shaman mask and the mask of the Olmec tribe in South Mexico are some of these. The Mexican Guerrero masks, like the masks of the Igbo, are used to enforce laws and exercise social and political control over the community.

Show examples of Igbo masks and their functions, for example, the *Aghogho mmuo* (the maiden spirit mask) which is used by the departed to speak for the last time to the living. It is also used to reconcile enemies or call offenders to order. When a villager is not behaving as (s)he should, the masks surround his/her dwelling during the night and threaten or maltreat the person until (s)he conforms.

Using a model for art criticism, lead the students through a discussion of the masks, analyzing, interpreting and evaluating, given the cultural contexts already discussed. Then have the students create a mask of their choice. The teacher should encourage the students to create masks that express something from their own culture as the Igbo mask carvers express something

200

from their culture. This is necessary because this whole concept of multi-cultural and cross-cultural art experience is not to reproduce or copy the mask of the Igbo; it is to make Igbo mask meaningful in the lives of the students.

Different materials should be made available for the students to use, for example, construction papers and paper bags could be used to fashion the masks while the students' imaginations are allowed to go riot with beads, strings, yarns, pebbles, small size boxes, and other found objects. The students could break boundaries, invent or push boundaries. Such endeavors will also call for the teacher adopting Eisner's flexible purposing approach. After the mask is completed, the teacher could have the students form "masquerade groups", bring old sheets or costumes from home or elsewhere, and enact masquerade performances. Have each group discuss its experience(s) and say which function(s) the masquerade was meant to perform and so on.

This provides a wonderful opportunity for cohesive learning that can be sparked as teachers work together with this cultural phenomenon of the mask. An English teacher could have the students write about masks from the experience of being the character that the mask conveys on them. I can just see teachers building a whole semester worth of work out of the experience of that central concept of the mask. I can see it working in history classes---the kinds of masks that these cultures wear, what the cultures were that these masks are from and exploring those cultures in Social Studies.

This, to me, is the kind of concept that makes for a very exciting curriculum for students, much more interesting than the kibbles and bits stuff that we tend to do, memorizing and regurgitating. It takes the frustration away from making instruction multicultural and makes teaching and learning more exciting and fun.

Conclusion

The success of multicultural education in the classrooms is contingent upon the attitudes and behaviors of classroom teachers (Rodriguez., 1983), therefore, to effectively teach in a multicultural classroom, teachers must first of all "examine, confront, and correct the prejudices they may have..., constantly monitor their feeling and attitudes towards different sociocultural groups.. and deal with their own biases in a positive, constructive manner" (Stuhr, et al., 1992, p. 19). This is essential because it will definitely take a convert to convincingly convert the natives. This does not in any way suggest that teachers must divorce themselves

202

from their own cultures, neither does it call for the students' rejection of their past and belief systems as Clark (1990) fears. The conversion is rather a mind set. to help the teacher and the children set their minds free and divest themselves of all pre-conceived notion about the people, and to help them understand, respect, and value the diversity of cultures without prejudice Clark (1990). This is necessary because, as Anderson (1991) observes, "what we hold to be significant--emotionally and intellectually---determines the course our learning will take" (p. 20).

Activities and questions for discussion

A.   Write down the different cultural celebrations that take place at your school. Identify the similarities and differences between these cultures.

B.   Using the Travel Agency Model, plan a trip to any culture of your choice.

C.   Design a lesson that makes cross-disciplinary and cross-cultural connections.

D.   How would you introduce the art of Native Americans to your students?

E.   What is the role of the teacher as ethnographer?

F.   Analyze the concept of "Teacher as Furniture Maker." What are its implications to multicultural education?

REFERENCES

Anderson, T. (1991). The content of art criticism. Art Education, 44 (1), 20.

Banks, J. A. (1997). Teaching strategies for ethnic studies (6 ed.). Boston: Allyn & Bacon.

Banks. J. A. (1994). Transforming the mainstream curriculum. Educational Leadership, 51(8), 4.

Baptiste, Jr. H. P. (1994). The multicultural environment of schools: Implications to leaders. In L. W. Hughes, (ed.) The principal as leader. New York: Macmillan.

Best, D. (1986). Culture-consciousness: Understanding the arts of other cultures. Journal of Art and Design Education, 5 (1, 2), 33-34.

Bolin, F. S. (1986). The community of scholars in supervision. A paper presented at the AERA, Teachers College, Columbia University.

Borich, G. D. (2000). Effective teaching methods (4th edition). New Jersey: Prentice Hall.

Boughton, D. (1986). How do we prepare art teachers for a multicultural society? Journal of Multi-cultural and Cross-cultural Research in Art Education, 4(1), 94-99.

Chalmers, G. F. (1992). The origins of racism in the public school art curriculum. Studies in Art Education,, 33(3), 134-143.

Chalmers, G. F. (1992). D.B.A.E. as multicultural education. Art Education 45 (3), 16.

Clark, G. (1990). Art in the schizophrenic fast lane: A response. Art Education 43 (6), 9-11.

Courtney, R. (1980). The crux of the cultural curriculum: The arts as anthropocentrism. In J. Condous, J. Howlette, and J. Skull, (Eds.), Arts in cultural diversity. Proceedings of the INSEA 23rd World Congress. New York: Holt, Rinehart and Winston.

DiBlasio, M. & Park, Y. (1983). Cultural identity and pride through art education: Viewpoint of a Korean-American immigrant community. Journal of Multicultural and Cross-cultural Research in Art Education, 1(1), 33-42.

Feldman. F. (1976). Art and the image of the self. Art Education, 29 (5), 10-12.

Gastor, J. (1984). Cultural awareness teaching techniques. Resource Handbook #4. Prolingua Associates.

Gay. G. (1986). Multicultural teacher education. In J. Banks and J. Lynch. (Eds.), Multicultural education in Western societies. London: Holt, Rinehart & Winston.

Glickman, C. (1985). Supervision of instruction: A developmental approach. Boston: Allyn & Bacon.

Grigsby, F. (1989). Emphasizing multicultural aspects in art education (Summary). Proceedings of a national invitational

206

conference (p. 105). Los Angeles, California: The Getty Center for Education in the Arts.

Grigsby, F. (1986). Using the arts to create bonds between people: The Phoenix experience. Journal of Multi-cultural and Cross-cultural Research in Art Education, 4(1), 17-29.

Guild, P. (1994) The culture/learning style connection. Educational Leadership, 51(8), 16.

Hamblen, K. A. (1986). A universal-relative approach to the study of cross-cultural art. Journal of Multi-cultural and Cross-cultural Research in Art Education, 4(1), 69-77.

Hazard, W. R. & Stent, M. D. (1973). Cultural pluralism and schooling: Some preliminary observations. In M. D. Stent, W. R. Hazard and H. N. Rivlin (Eds.), Cultural pluralism in education: A mandate for change. New York: Appleton-Century-Crofts.

James, R. L. (1978). Multicultural education: NCATE standard rationale. Journal of Teacher Education, 29 (1), 13-20.

Katter. F. (1991). Meeting the challenge of cultural diversity. Visual Arts Research, 17(2), 28-32.

Ladson-Billings. G. (1994). What we can learn from multicultural education research. Educational Leadership, 51(8), pp. 22-24.

Lovano-Kerr, J (1985). Cultural diversity and art education: A global perspective. Journal of Multi-cultural and Cross-cultural Research in Art Education, 3 (1), 25.

207

Manning, M. & Baruth, L. G. (1991). Appreciating cultural diversity in the classroom. Kappa Delta Pi Record 27 (4), 104.

McFee, I. K. (1980). Cultural influences on aesthetic experience. Arts in cultural diversity. Proceedings of the INSEA world congress. Australia: Holt, Rinehart & Winston.

Nadaner, D. (1985). The art teacher as cultural mediator. Journal of Multicultural and Cross-cultural Research in Art Education, 3 (1), 51-55.

Ogbu, J. U. (1992). Understanding cultural diversity and learning Educational Researcher, 21(8), 5-14.

Reck, M. U, Reck, G. G., & Keefe, S. (1993). Implications of teachers' perceptions of students in an Appalachian school system. Journal of Research and Development in Education, 26 (2), 117-121.

Rodriguez, F. (1983). Education in a multicultural society. Washington, DC: University Press of America.

Sergiovanni, T. & Starratt, R. J. (1993). Supervision: A redefinition. New York: McGraw Hill.

Short, E. C. (ed.) (1991). Forms of curriculum inquiry. New York: State University Press.

Smith, R. A. (1980). Celebrating the arts in their cultural diversity: Some wrong and right ways to do it. Arts in cultural diversity. Proceedings of the INSEA 23rd world congress. Australia: Holt, Rinehart & Winston.

Kilborne B. and Langness, L. E. (eds.). (1987). Culture and human nature. University of Chicago Press.

Spradley J. P. (1979). The ethnographic interview. New York: Harcourt Brace.

Stuhr, P. L., Petrovich-Nwaniki, L., & Wasson, R. (1992). Curriculum guidelines for the multicultural art classroom. Art Education, 45 (1), 16-24.

Tomhave, R. D. (1992). Value bases underlying conceptions of multicultural education: An analysis of selected literature in art education. Studies in Art Education 34 (1), 48-60.

Ubben, C. G. & Hughes, L. W. (1992). The Principal: Creative Leadership for effective schools. Boston: Allyn and Bacon.

Yoshitomi, G. (1989). Emphasizing multicultural aspects in art education. [Summary]. Proceedings of a national invitational conference (pp. 105-107). Los Angeles, California: The Getty Center for Education in the Arts.

Zimmerman, E. (1990). Questions about multi-culture and art education or "I'll never forget the day M'Blawi stumbled on the work of the post impressionists". Art Education, 43(6), 8-24.

CHAPTER 11

Urban or Suburb- The Issues Remain the Same

Mary M. Addison, Ed. D.
Dolores A. Westmoreland, Ed. D.
Houston Independent School District
Houston, TX

If you inquire what people are like here, I must answer, "The same as everywhere!" Johannn Von Goethe, The Sorrows of Young Werther, 1787. Quoted in Bartlett's Familiar Quotations, p. 349.

The sentiments expressed by the writer, Goethe, over two hundred years ago are just as timely today. Regardless of the size of the school district or the schools within those districts, the issues, which face the educational administrators, are the same.

With the publication of *The Nation at Risk*, school administrators were challenged to become introspective and to address topics perceived by the public to be of concern. Accountability became the buzzword of those who sought school reforms and changes in the status quo of public education. No longer was the public content to allow the schools to operate *in loco parentis* with little regard for student or parental rights. In fact, the public schools were expected to provide many roles

211

usually reserved for the family unit or religious institutions such as character and sex education or early childhood and family support programs. Unlike our foreign contemporaries, American public schools are expected, "to be all things to all people."

The mission statement of most public schools has proposed two major objectives for their charges: (1) to stimulate the desire and provide instruction for sound scholarly achievement; and (2) to provide an atmosphere conducive for the development of interpersonal expertise required for societal entrance. Today's school administrators must strive to achieve these lofty aims while, at the same time, addressing the reality of school management.

The information presented in this chapter will provide educators with an overview some of the common issues facing educators in both urban and suburban school districts, which will be discussed in succeeding chapters of this book.

Student Enrollment Struggle

There can be no school without having a student population. In the past, the public schools enjoyed a monopoly status and parents were forced to accept the schools' dictates and curriculum because only the very wealthy could afford the luxury of private education.

Today, the public schools are faced with an enrollment dilemma with the advent of numerous academic campus choices such as charter schools, magnet schools, as well as private religious and secular schools. Since the majority of school funding is determined by school enrollment, schools are faced with building a better mousetrap to entice student participation.

Magnet Schools

Within a given school system, schools are competing for membership by creating magnet schools which feature a given program of study. Students who profess an interest in pursuing a given program of study will vie for enrollment in a given magnet school. At one school district in the South, parents of elementary-age children have been known to spend several nights and days encamped outside the school building, which features Montessori training, to secure placement for their children. In New York City, one of their magnet schools has twelve thousand applications for the freshman class of one thousand each year.

When parents believe that a given school has a superior instructional program, they will forsake their local school in pursuit of acceptance into the believed better school. In our own school district, we have watched with amusement the extreme measures

213

utilized by parents to enroll their children in a preferred school. One parent, utilizing the current technology, gave a bogus address, which was in the desired school zone. Because he knew that the school checked telephone numbers as well as addresses, he had a telephone installed in home of a friend located in the school zone, which would provide the correct telephone prefix. The telephone number was perpetually assigned to call forwarding, thus, when the school called the number in their attendance zone, it was forwarded to the actual phone located in the home of the student not in the attendance zone!

Charter Schools

The establishment of charter schools has experienced an increased growth from one in 1992 to more than 800 in early 1998. Charter schools, established and authorized by state agencies and/or school districts, are not regulated by the constraints of the local school district. These schools are usually established to provide service to a given population and have an innovative curriculum. The charters promise to provide academic results, in the form of higher standardized test scores, with their enrollees in exchange for less structured regulation. Because they are licensed by the state or local district, they receive the funding for students from the state agencies. This reduces revenue from the public school budget.

Charter school founders are usually educators, parents, or organizations. Educators with a certain educational philosophical vision could establish a charter school. Such was the creation of the Kipp Academy in Houston, Texas, by two young elementary school teachers who had entered the teaching profession through the Teach for America program. These young men were so successful with their school, that they have established a second one in New York City and were featured recently on a segment of *60 Minutes*.

Parents have also established charter schools because they believe the education obtained from the public schools does not meet their expectations for their children. Often, these parents share a common political or religious priority and desire this view to be expressed through the school curriculum. Similarly, some organizations will request a charter to assist a given school population. Some charters are established to address at-risk students, while others seek to educate certain ethnicities.

Home Schooling

Another group, which is removing students from the public schools, are students who are being schooled in their homes. There are many parents who have the time and expertise to teach their children at home. Many of these form alliances with other parents and they share their expertise. On any given day, a group of home-schooled children may attend an algebra class in a given home, while others are studying science with a parent at the local science museum. While these parents do not receive any state or federal funding for their children, the allocation for these home-school students is denied the public schools.

Public school administrators must advertise their instructional programs and their schools to attract potential students. As in the business world, there is no better advertisement than a satisfied customer. When parents speak positively about a given school program to other parents, their influence can be as powerful as Oprah Winfrey recommending a given novel for her viewers' reading!

Financing the Schools

In addition to having curriculum and instructional expertise, today's school administrator must also possess fiscal acumen. Each new school year the school districts are given

216

mandates from the state and federal agencies to provide new programs and services for their students. Unfortunately, the funding for these innovations must be provided by the local school districts. Since the local school districts are bound by law regarding raising the tax base to support such innovations, they must devise other methods of funding.

Grants

One method of funding programs is through grant writing. Many school districts have established grant-writing departments to assist the individual schools and the entire school district in securing funding by this process. Care must be taken to word the grant application properly or the application will be rejected. The program being touted for the funds must be very innovative and creative to secure the money. Often restrictions are placed upon the funds with regard to how the money may be allocated. Similarly, certain vendors may be designated from whom materials may be purchased with the grant money. Additionally, schools receiving the grant funds must document how the money was spent and provide documentation of accountability regarding the success of the given program. This is usually done by standardized testing results. However, to the persistent administrator, funds can be secured for school projects through the writing of grants.

Business Partners

In recent years, securing a business partner for the school has proven to be fiscally rewarding. How fortunate is the school that has a business partner volunteer time and money without solicitation! For the majority of schools, the schools must request this business-education collaboration.

The business partner must believe that his time and funding will be beneficial to both his company and the school being served. Many companies are willing to finance school programs if they are convinced of the necessity and relevance. The school must be willing to abide by some restrictions by the business partner.

One middle school had a bank as a business partner. Among the services provided by the bank was to allow its personnel to visit the school weekly to tutor students in the school's reading room. The bank branches provided reading material for the reading room such as magazines and books. Additionally, the bank employees collected thousands of dollars of school supplies to be distributed to the students during the school year. Likewise, the bank provided funding and transportation for

218

the students to attend cultural events such as the ballet and dramatic performances.

The school administration must be willing to collaborate with the business partner to assure the success of the given program. In the case of the above-mentioned bank, the middle school administrator had to arrange for the students to report to the reading room promptly for their tutorial sessions with the bank personnel weekly.

Community Partners

There may be community organizations, which will provide funding for school programs. Some of the organizations such as the Lions' Club, Rotary Club, and others are willing to assist schools with projects. In Houston, the city will assist an elementary school with play equipment and building a campus park, which can be used by the community during after school and on weekends. The elementary schools must provide half the funding for the park and the city will match those funds. This collaboration is beneficial to both the school and the community.

At one high school, the local ministerial association provides a banquet each spring for the students who successfully passed the state-mandated examination for graduation. This effort was the result of the high school principal initiating an annual ministerial breakfast to secure support of the community churches.

School administrators must seek the support of outside agencies for additional funding. Some school districts have departments dedicated for just this purpose. Many companies have money allocated in their budgets for educational support. The school or school district administrator should contact the personnel in the company at the beginning of the company's fiscal year to have funds allocated for a given educational project.

Stretching the Budget

As school districts are becoming more decentralized and the burden for school finance becomes the responsibility of the site-based administrator, the issue of school budget becomes more relevant. The school principal must disperse the budgeted money among programs, materials, and facilities with the wisdom of Solomon.

Many school campuses have site-based decision committees which assist the principal in determining the expenditure of school funds; however, the ultimate responsibility lies with the principal. The principal must be certain that the funds are spent in the correct designations according to the law.

Principals who are not frugal with their budgeted funds and do not amortize them over the entire school year could find themselves unable to provide services and materials at the close of the school year. Teachers are seldom very understanding when told by the principal that there are no funds remaining in the budget to purchase copying paper for the Xerox machine!

Staff Selection

One cannot have a school without a professional teaching staff and the school-site administrator must select from the applicants presented the best match for the given position. As every administrator knows, thorough knowledge of one's subject matter does not necessarily qualify a candidate to be a superior instructor.

Characteristics of Successful Teachers

Prior to conducting interviews for a given position, the school principal has considered characteristics, which the suitable applicant must have to fulfill the obligations of the position. While these desirable traits are intangible, it is possible to design interview questions, which will demonstrate them.

221

Possibly, the principal traits sought in a teacher would include these:

1. Positive attitude: Everyone responds more readily to an attitude of acceptance than one of rejection. A teacher can be stern and still maintain a positive attitude. Since students mirror the attitude of the instructor, one who constantly projects a positive demeanor within the classroom will encourage greater student participation.

2. Respectful: Students must perceive that they are respected by the adult in charge of the classroom. Because students often operate emotionally, they will react to any demonstration of disrespect from their teacher. These reactions usually earn the students an opportunity to visit the office of the assistant principal.

3. Tolerant: Students will follow suggestions more readily if they believe that the adult making the suggestions accepts them as a person and does not consider them to be inferior.

4. Empathic: The successful teacher must demonstrate empathy for the student's perception of a situation, regardless of how insignificant it appears to the instructor.

5. Supportive: Students must believe that their teacher

supports them personally and they will work diligently for him or her in the classroom.

6.   Attentive: Teachers must be active listeners while students are expressing themselves and they will observe dialogue clues to the students' feelings.

Interviewing Applicants

With the use of strategic interview questions, the school principal can secure pertinent information from the applicant and discern evidence of the above listed characteristics.

The interview questions are usually of the open or closed variety. Closed questions may be answered with a simple "yes" or "no", whereas, open-ended questions allow the respondent to extend his answer. For example, asking the applicant if he graduated from a given university could be answered with a simple affirmative or negative response. Asking the applicant to enumerate some of her classroom rules would provide an opportunity for an extended response.

The interviewer should establish a climate of trust with initial questions by posing background questions. Posing hypothetical situational questions would allow the principal to see evidence of many of the above-mentioned characteristics as well as how the applicant might handle some potential situation in the classroom. An example of such a question would be "What would you do, Mrs. Smith, if one of your students came to class without his text book and materials?".

While there is no given set of questions, which will guarantee selection of the perfect applicant for a given position, using the questioning, suggestions presented should narrow the subjectivity and allow the principal to make an intelligent choice.

Nurturing Success

The principal is the acknowledged instructional leader of the campus and, as such, must motivate and encourage teaches, students, and staff to achieve success. It is a well-established axiom that an individual must motivate himself or herself. Conditions can be created which will cause the individual to desire a positive goal and work conscientiously to obtain it.

A successful sales person not only demonstrates a thorough knowledge of the product being sold, but also exhibits a contagious enthusiasm for the product. Schoolteachers must be like the used car salesman, in a television commercial, who jumps excitedly on the hood of an automobile while extolling its virtues. The teacher who does not demonstrate a love for his or her subject and generate an enthusiastic class presentation will have a classroom of apathetic learners. Similarly, the school principal must create a desire for achievement within the teachers through meaningful staff development programs.

Staff Development

With the increased emphasis being placed upon accountability, it is imperative that staff development programs be designed, which address the skills and information which the students being served need to know to complete the grade or course successfully. With this being identified, the staff development program must consider what knowledge the teachers must acquire and what expertise they must demonstrate to enable their students to achieve the desired goals. Having considered the knowledge and expertise required for the teaching staff, the staff developers must determine which learning processes must be implemented to assist the teaching staff in acquiring the necessary knowledge and expertise to successfully instruct the student body.

Staff development programs must align with the desired accountability expectations. The teachers should not spend daydreaming while some loquacious consultant articulates her qualifications to instruct the staff regarding some strategy or

225

technique having little or no bearing upon the district's instructional goals. The programs should encourage the teachers to apply the new knowledge and expertise acquired in their lessons and assesses the influence on instruction.

With successful, relevant, staff development programs, the statewide test results will produce the expected results.

Student Motivation

The saying, "Your attitude determines your altitude," certainly applies to student achievement. An unmotivated student with a negative attitude is not going to assimilate any of the instruction given during a class period. As previously stated, one cannot make a student achieve; he must desire and want to achieve himself, however, there are motivational strategies which could inspire the student to seek success.

Psychologists have classified motivation as being extrinsic and intrinsic. A student who is intrinsically motivated will desire to learn information for the self-satisfaction of acquiring knowledge, while the extrinsically motivated student will learn information to achieve some prize or external recognition. Elementary teachers are the greatest extrinsic motivators with their little stars, stickers, and check marks placed on the student products! While secondary school teachers would argue that their charges should be intrinsically motivated to learn the information for a standardized examination, reality dictates that the students have not matured sufficiently to achieve this status.

Everyone appreciates being rewarded for effort, even teachers. At a high school in Houston, the assistant principal was responsible for monitoring the teachers standing at their doors between classes on a given floor of the building. The principal instructed that letters of reprimand be issued to those not complying with the directive. Wishing to make the directive a positive consequence rather than a negative, she created a drawstring bag and filled it with candy. At different periods during the day, if the teachers were outside their doors as directed, they received a piece of candy. Soon, all of the teachers were standing at their doors waiting for their reward. One day a student approached the assistant principal requesting that she give a science instructor a piece of candy. The student said, " Mrs. X missed the candy run because she was in the classroom answering my question." While intrinsically, the teachers should have been motivated to obey the directive to stand at their door between classes, the extrinsic motivation of receiving a candy treat certainly got them on their feet!

One middle school principal promised his students that he would operate from the roof of his school building an entire day if they improved significantly on the state-mandated achievement test. When the students complied, he fulfilled his promise and he worked the entire day on the roof! His picture was in the local newspaper showing him at a desk on the roof.

When a high school principal promised all students achieving academic recognition on the state-mandated examination required for graduation a letter jacket, the school achieved exemplary status from the state for their percentage of students passing the examination on the first attempt. The attitude of the student body changed from, "I have many more times to try to pass the examination before I graduate," to "I passed the examination, but I am upset because I did not achieve academic recognition."

What motivates one group of students may not work with another group. Educators must decide what will motivate their population to success and apply that reward. As the Nike ad proclaims, "Just Do It."

Student Attendance

The saying, "What if an extravagant party was planned and no one came?" certainly applies to student attendance. A teacher can prepare the most creative lesson and have the most imaginative manipulatives to emphasize the skill, but if there are no students attending the class, the effort is wasted. Student attendance is a significant threat to both the economics and academics of a school system. The majority of the schools are funded based upon the average daily attendance of the school enrollment, therefore, a habitually absent student can significantly lower the attendance average of the school. Additionally, it is a proven axiom that absence from school will result in academic failure. With school accreditation dependent upon statewide-standardized examinations, the students must be present to receive adequate instruction to successfully pass.

In the good old days, a school administrator would just withdraw a habitually absent student, which would improve the attendance average calculation. Today, with the emphasis upon dropout accountability and the business world's complaint of unqualified, uneducated job applicants, this procedure is no longer feasible.

Elementary schools enjoy the higher percentage of attendance because the younger children are eager learners and their working parents have a free child-care facility during the day. Secondary schools experience a higher percentage of absenteeism because the students have achieved a greater independence and are not afraid to leave school and travel around the city or town unsupervised.

The majority of school districts have established an attendance department with staff who visit the homes of truant students. The parent of the chronically under-aged truant student is referred to the local courts for judgment.

While the courts are specific that it is the obligation of the parent or guardian to assure school attendance, the schools must devise strategies to encourage attendance. Some states have established a minimum number of days which a student may have an unexcused absence. Students exceeding this number will forfeit their credit in the class, or be subject to grade retention. Even the threat of credit loss does not deter many students from skipping classes.

To encourage attendance, some school districts have allowed high school students to be exempt from their final examinations if they do not exceed a given number of absences. Other schools have offered various prizes for good attendance while some classroom teachers give grade points for class attendance.

It is imperative that the schools secure parental support in the attendance effort. Teachers should be encouraged to communicate with parents when the student demonstrates a consistent pattern of absenteeism. The "out of sight, out of mind" attitude upon the part of many teachers cannot be tolerated. Administrators must hold the classroom teacher accountable for notifying parents of truant students and not expect the attendance office to maintain the sole responsibility for notification. The expression, "A mind is a terrible thing to waste," certainly applies to the truant student whose intellect is not being stimulated because of his absence from class.

At-Risk Students

Unfortunately, no utopian schools exist where all of the students arrive daily with all of their materials and books eager for learning. In every school there is the problem of the non-motivated, marginal students who will choose not to remain enrolled in school and complete the requirements for high school graduation. The marginal or at-risk student is usually in the bottom quarter of his class scholastically when grade point averages are calculated. Characteristics of these students could be classified into five domains—familial-environmental, psychological, behavioral, social, and academic.

Familial-environmental

"God gives us relatives; thank God, we can choose our friends," wrote Addison Mizner in The Cynics' Calendar (1986, p. 153). There are many familial-environmental situations, which might contribute to the marginal student. One of the primary reasons given is the absence of a nuclear family. Today's students do not return from school daily to a home similar those depicted in the fifties sitcom such as Ozzie and Harriet. They are the children of a single parent, usually a mother, who often works extended hours and is not home to direct homework assignments or encourage recreational reading through library usage.

Often, whether the student has one parent or two, the student is unsupervised until the early evening because of lengthy employment requirements. Left alone to his own entertainment, the student will watch television or play video games- neither of which requires any higher order thinking capability.

A student whose parents and siblings are poorly educated has little motivation or encouragement to remain in school. Often, these children are required to work long hours to contribute to the family income. Additionally, many of these students experience a high mobility rate because their families change locations to avail themselves of the special discounts given to first-time tenants.

Psychological

Because these students experience a feeling of low self-esteem, they will demonstrate characteristics of alienation, which manifest into an acceptance of failure. These same students will verbalize a belief that the administration and teaching staff have little regard for them, personally, and/or whether they are in attendance at school. Having a lack of definitive goals, these marginal students are prime candidates for school withdrawal.

Behavioral

It is often the overt behavior of the at-risk student, which identifies him to the classroom teacher and school staff. These are the students who are diagnosed as being hyperactive and having an attention deficit because they are unable to tolerate highly structured activities. The school nurse is busy dispensing the medication of these children daily to curtail their hyper-kinetic manifestations. The parents of these students receive numerous visits from the truancy officer because of their high rate of absenteeism. Having a lack of respect for authority, these marginal learners become disruptive in the classroom and could face suspension at least once a semester. Likewise, their disregard for authority is observed by their choice of school attire and grooming. These are the ones stereotypically labeled as being "punkers" or "Goths" by traditional scholars.

Social

Since these individuals choose to participate in few extra-curricular school activities, they have ample time to become involved in such illicit non-school activities as gang membership. Having an excess of unsupervised time, these at-risk students could have a potential affiliation with drugs as either the seller or the consumer. Unfortunately, many will involve themselves in other avenues of crime and face possible incarceration or lengthy probation. As McKenzie so aptly hypothesized, "many of the dropouts go from school to night court." (McKenzie, 1980, p. 460.)

Academic

Students who qualify as academically at-risk experience difficulty in basic skills' foundations and their reading level does not correlate to their grade level. Because reading comprehension

234

is an acute problem for these students, they experience a discrepancy between their intellectual ability and their academic performance. Often the student is not a native English speaker and has difficulty communicating and understanding his subjects.

Motivation of At-Risk Students

Educators have offered divergent opinions regarding appropriate educational prescriptions for the academically ailing at-risk student. Since the decision to withdraw from school often generates from classroom experiences, school personnel are encouraged to adopt a new paradigm with regard to classroom instruction. First, staff development programs should instruct teachers to identify potential at-risk characteristics. Second, teachers must adopt teaching methodologies, which appeal to the divergent learning styles of the class members. Third, classroom teachers must understand and implement positive motivational strategies, which appeal to the diverse membership of the class. There is not an administrator in the United States who has not heard from a recalcitrant student the reason for noncompliance or failure was a personality conflict with the teacher. Fourth, and certainly not the least in importance, is a perception of student

235

success by the teachers. All students will learn if they perceive that the instruction is interesting, relevant, and inspirational.

To achieve this goal and reduce the dropout statistics for these marginal students, teachers and administrators must engage in meaningful planning. As the saying goes, "If we do not educate these students in school; we will be paying for their incarceration in prison."

Serving Special Populations

While private schools can determine their school population by choice, public schools are dedicated to the philosophy, like the lines from the famous poem by the poet, Emma Lazarus, that all students are welcomed through its portals to be educated.

Limited English Speaking Students

Since the United States has been called "the melting pot of nations," one of the special populations, which must be educated, is a student for whom English is not their primary language. The number of Limited English Proficiency students in the United States has grown dramatically in the last decade. A recent national survey has shown that there are over 3 million students in grades K-12 who have Limited English Proficiency.

In 1968, Congress passed the Bilingual Education Act, or Title VII, to provide federal funding for bilingual programs. It has undergone many revisions, but recently the Office of Civil Rights has visited many states and school districts to ascertain that these students are being served sufficiently.

All schools are expected to survey every student and his parent, upon his initial entry into a school, to determine if English as a Second Language services are to be provided. Once the student is determined to require these services, the school is obligated to enroll him into the program after being tested to determine his program placement.

Because additional funding is provided for the education of the Limited English Proficiency student by the federal government, specific guidelines must be maintained which necessitate careful documentation. The information about the student is maintained in a folder, which must follow the student as he matriculates from one school campus to another.

Students must remain in the ESL program until standardized testing indicates their removal. The parent of an ESL student may request that his student not participate by signing a waiver each school year during a conference with the school administrator.

The teacher of ESL or bilingual students must have taken college courses, which will certify them in the teaching methodology. Should the school not have a certified instructor, it must submit documentation stating this fact.

When the LEP students are enrolled in the ESL classes, they are concentrating upon learning the English language itself. When they are in the subject content classrooms, the language is used as a means of learning about the given subject and as a means of communicating, analyzing, synthesizing, and evaluating information gained from listening, reading, and engaging in learning experiences.

Recently, there has been some disagreement regarding the instruction of the LEP students. Some educators believe that placing the LEP students in a separate classroom serves to isolate them from the regular population and hinders their acquisition of English. Others feel that the total immersion of the students into the content classrooms would frustrate the ESL student and, experiencing a sense of failure, might lead to withdrawal from school. Regardless of the philosophy of instructional presentation, it is the obligation of the schools to prepare these students to meet the challenges of the future armed with the best language skills possible.

Special Education Students

Among the student population of any school are those with an identifiable disability, which impacts their learning. With the passage of Public Law 94-142, the Education for All Handicapped Children Act in 1975, and the subsequent revision in 1990 renaming it The Individuals with Disabilities Act (IDEA), students with special needs have been provided access to public schools and their classrooms.

As with the Bilingual Education Act, the federal government has given instructions regarding the identification, placement, and instruction of the students with disabilities. Intensive documentation must be completed for each student in the special education program. As with the LEP folder, the special education folder is transferred from one campus to another with the student.

Prior to the implementation of IDEA, the parents were not as involved with the decision-making regarding their children. This exclusion resulted in much litigation against the school districts. Now, the parents are considered equal partners with the

239

schools in all decisions concerning their offspring. Additionally, IDEA granted parents greater rights such as examination of their child's records, reevaluation of their child's educational program, obtaining independent evaluations, and notification of any program changes.

Parents collaborate with their child's teachers, specialists, and administration to determine the child's specialized Individual Educational Plan (IEP), which should afford successful completion of his schooling. These plans outline the teaching modifications necessary for the student to achieve in a given course. Teachers must provide documentation that these are being followed for each student taught.

The IDEA revision decreed that all children with disabilities be served in the least restrictive environment. No longer are the students segregated in rooms away from the general school population, but now, where possible, included in the general education classrooms. Interaction with the general regular education school population should allow students to sharpen their socialization skills, maximize their strengths and interests in the learning process, achieve independence within the school and community, thus, becoming contributing participants.

This declaration has generated much controversy among the educational community. Teachers in the general education classes, reluctant to change their classroom presentations, complain that it is difficult to adjust one's lesson to accommodate the level of instruction required by special education students. Since inclusion of special education students into the general population is relatively new, one must not be hasty in rendering a decision regarding its effectiveness. The instructional reorganization by the general education teacher should prove beneficial to all students serviced since the educational strategies being addressed to the special education students can be utilized on the entire class.

School principals, who accept student diversity, can encourage their faculty to accept the challenge of including students with disabilities into the general population. Having high expectation for all of their students, these principals can insist that their teachers provide comparable curricula for both groups by monitoring the lesson plans and classroom presentations.

Gifted and Talented Students

Often, students considered to be gifted and talented are ignored by the educational community because they are occupied with addressing the needs of the special education student, the limited English-speaking student, or the at-risk student. Because these students are believed to exhibit a potential for high-levels of accomplishment independently, many educators do not provide an adequate support system for these superior students. Many instructors of gifted students believe that little instruction is required for them to comprehend the skill being presented. Additionally, having the philosophy of "more is better," teachers will reward these intellectuals with a plethora of busy work assignments.

Some school administrators have been reluctant to group these students in a specific tract of curriculum for fear of creating an elitist attitude among the participants. Some teachers are reluctant to lead such an identified group for fear of being shown to be intellectually inferior to their students.

The Javits Gifted and Talented Students Act, passed in 1988 and reauthorized in 1994, has provided grant subsidies for instructional materials and teacher staff development to improve the instruction of the gifted students. In 1993, Ross edited a report for the U.S. Department of Education, National excellence: A care for Developing America's Talent. This document increased the public and educational community's awareness regarding the identification and education of gifted children.

Today, many states have programs to identify the gifted students, train the teachers to serve this population, and to provide teaching materials for the classrooms.

Evaluating Student Performance

It is a rare newspaper day when there is not one article or "Letter to the Editor" which does not address school accountability. The current benchmark for such measurement is the student results on a given standardized test. The probable reason for this evaluation is that the public understands numbers and cannot observe the intangible successes being achieved such as increasing self-esteem, instilling character traits, or developing independent thinking. Many states have mandated examinations, which measure student achievement in the elementary and middle school grades and must be passed to graduate from high school.

The perception of school personnel today towards the standardized accountability mantle being thrust upon them is similar to the school described in the Dr. Seuss book, *Hooray for Diffendoofer Day* (1995):

> "All schools for miles and miles around
> Must take a special test.
> To see who's learning such and such—
> To see which school's the best.
> If our small school does not do well,

Then it will be torn down,
And you will have to go to school
In dreary Flobbertown."

Administrators, teachers, and students experience concern, like the above-mentioned school, to perform successfully on these examinations. Millions of dollars of teaching materials are offered annually to provide the solution for the standardized dilemma. The school administrator must decide which program will best address the requirements for his or her particular student population.

Regardless of the intense debate regarding the use of standardized testing for accountability, the school, whose students successfully master the examination, is prompt to use this fact in their solicitation for new students.

Teacher Liability and Student Rights

In today's society, where the number of lawyers appears to equal the number of stars in the sky, there is always some barrister ready to assist an angry patron in suing the schools, the administration or the teachers.   Often school personnel bring litigation upon themselves through ignorance of the law, poor documentation, or poor judgment.

244

Teachers are reminded each school year that proper documentation is crucial in all written records because these items could be used in a court of law. At the high school level, where parents are desperate to salvage some lost high school credit, teachers are exhorted to have accurate, detailed records in their grade books regarding grades and attendance. Recently, many teachers and schools have been challenged in court for the failure to provide adequate instruction to graduating students. Having thorough lesson plans, a well-documented grade book, and, in the case of a special education student, well-documented modification implementation, can assist teachers in avoiding academic challenges. Many schools have definitive policies regarding the notification of academic failure and repeated absences to parents. Failure to provide such notification could result in the passing of a failing student.

The beginning teacher should be instructed by the school administration regarding the policies of the school system and the local campus. Often, their errors in judgment result from a lack of information regarding the policies regarding supervision and discipline.

The unintentional violation of student rights could pose a potential lawsuit. Search and seizure are two of the most

245

challenged actions in the court. Assistant principals must be aware of all discipline procedures, especially those regarding special education students.

Child abuse and sexual harassment are prominent among the court cases being tried today. Teachers and administrators are required by law to report the suspicion of child abuse and sexual harassment. Dismissing a student's complaint regarding either situation as being minor could result in serious liability for a teacher or administrator. Additionally, teachers must be professional in their relationships with students. Frivolous remarks could be interpreted as being either sexual harassment or abusive to the student.

Clear communication with the parents can often reduce the threat of litigation. The teacher who has communicated with a parent, either verbally or with written progress reports throughout the six weeks or the semester, will not be challenged regarding student assessment. School administrators have no problem defending their teachers who have well-documented evidence for a given grade. Additionally, the teacher who conducts a parent conference with a caring, empathic, respectful attitude will have little repercussions at the close of the conference from the parent.

246

School personnel must remember that without the children of these parents, they would be unemployed!

School Security

The recent violent attacks on school campuses across the nation have increased the public awareness for school safety and security measures. The public is often convinced by the extensive news media coverage of a violent event that all public schools are bastions of danger. Nothing could be further from the truth, because the majority of schools across the nation have safe, orderly campuses with few students observed outside the classroom during the school day.

Schools are very cognizant of their responsibility to provide protection for the students they serve. The majority of school districts have established security departments with police officers located on school campuses and patrolling school perimeters.

Technology has become an integral part of the security procedures on the local school campus. Schools have installed security cameras inside and outside the buildings to record activity. This has diminished the vandalism and acts of violence because the students know their actions are being recorded. Many schools have installed metal detection devices similar to those in the local airports to check for weapons. Most school districts have a zero tolerance policy towards any type of weapon and students, who defy this mandate, are immediately subject to expulsion.

Gang and drug awareness seminars are provided for the teaching staff and many school districts have substance abuse monitors located on the senior high school campus for prevention information and identification of offenders. As with the weapons infraction, drug consumption is usually a zero-tolerance offense in most school districts.

Many school districts have a collaborative relationship with the local law enforcement agencies to assist with student offenders. Many cities have curfew violations during the school day and issue citations to students on the streets and in the shopping malls who are not accompanied by their parents.

Schools must solicit the cooperation of their community in providing security and crime prevention. One urban high school enlisted the aid of the community in petitioning the city government to close a park located across the street from the campus during the school day. The park had been inhabited during the day by drug dealers and posed a threat to students entering the school campus.

Because the school campus is a microcosm of the surrounding community, and violence is prevalent within the community, students will reflect the actions on campus observed in the community. School personnel must provide a variety of preventive measures, both physical and educational, which will reduce the opportunity for turbulence.

Technological Advancements

The Internet has reduced the world's distance to a click of a mouse. Students can visit exotic locations, in living color, and chat with its inhabitants through the marvels of technology. In fact, there is so much technology available to today's students, the schools are working diligently to update curricular offerings. The student enrolled in the auto technology course must be prepared to understand the intricate working of the computer, since the majority of today's vehicles are computer operated.

Since today's generation of learners have played video and computer games since they were old enough to hold a joy stick or grasp a mouse, educators must change their paradigm of instruction to meet the challenge of this new learning modality. Today, there is a wonderful opportunity to present learning through the media of information given on CD ROMs, computer assisted instruction, and interactive learning via the Internet. Teachers must be willing to attend workshops and college courses to update their knowledge of the new equipment being utilized in the various classrooms.

Community, School, and Parent Dynamics

Schools are no longer an impenetrable fortress resistant to the outside assistance from parents and the community. As the African proverb states that, "It takes a whole village to raise a child," so schools must solicit the cooperation and form a partnership with the parents and community to educate the students being served.

Partnerships flourish when they are founded upon mutual trust and respect for the other's values. With the majority of today's students being non-white, it is imperative that the schools change the minority parents' perception from one of alienation and indifference to that of warmth and cooperation. Many of the minority parents may feel unwelcome on the campus because of differences in education, employment, or ethnicity when compared to school personnel. Additionally, the parents may perceive a psychological barrier to exist between the school personnel and themselves because the school had not embraced the community and its residents. The majority of school personnel do not reside in the community being served by the school and are rarely seen the community except when traveling to and from school.

Educators need parental assistance to encourage academic achievement, reinforce discipline, and support school attendance and remaining in school. Schools should survey the community and provide activities, which will encourage parents to visit the schools. Schools could offer classes in ESL mastery and GED studies for parents requiring these services. Teaching parents to master the operation of computers would be helpful in providing a skill for future employment. The more educated that the parents become, the greater will be their contribution to the school.

Seeking volunteers among the parental and community members for school activities strengthens the bond between the school and its patrons. When parents volunteer their time for an hour or a day each week, it provides them with a sense of purpose and ownership of the school. They will be the first to support a project of the school because they can identify with the school staff. Likewise, the school staff should be encouraged to participate in the activities held in the community such as religious programs, cultural events, and holiday festivities. When the students observe the school staff attending community functions, it

251

forms a bond of collaboration, which should be seen in the classrooms.

The welcome mat must be perceived by parents and community residents to be present at the neighborhood school at all times, or they will enroll their offspring in a school across town having a perceived friendlier climate!

Summary

The school superintendent supervising a school district of 1,000 students or 100,000 students and the school-site administrator serving a school of 300 students or 3000 students will face the common task of resolving the issues presented in this chapter.

The successful resolution will not depend upon the size of the district or campus nor its wealth, but upon the collaboration between all stakeholders in the educational institution— administrators, teachers, parents, community members, and students. As with the maxim, "United, we stand; divided, we fall."

References

Aiello, J., & Bullock, L. M. (1999). Building commitment to responsible inclusion. <u>Preventing School Failure, 43,</u> 99-102.

Anderson, M. A. (1999). The media center and the Internet: Selection, supervision and staff development. <u>Multimedia Schools, 6,</u> 24-27.

Bakken, T., & Kortering, L. (1999). The constitutional and statutory obligations of schools to prevent students with disabilities from dropping out. <u>Remedial and Special Education, 20,</u> 360-366.

Chamot, A., & O'Malley, J. M. (1994). The CALLA handbook. New York: Addison-Wesley Publishers.

Conderman, G., & Nelson, N. (1999). A better IDEA for parents, students, and educators. <u>Kappa Delta Pi Record, 35,</u> 170-172.

Day, C. W. (1999). Technology's role in security. <u>American School and University, 72,</u> 54-55.

Dunlap, C. Z., & Alva, S. A. (1999). Redefining school and community relations: Teachers' perceptions of parents as participants and stakeholders. <u>Teacher Education Quarterly, 4,</u> 123-133.

Feldman, S. (1998). School safety: We're all responsible. <u>American Teacher, 83,</u> 5-6.

Gameros, P. (1995). The visionary principal and inclusion of students with disabilities. NASSP Bulletin, 79, 15-17.

Griffin, R., & Davalos, G. (1999). The impact of teachers' individualized practices on gifted students in rural, heterogeneous classrooms. Roeper Review, 21, 308-314.

Hirsch, S., & Sparks, D. (1999). Staff development resolutions for the next millennium. High School Magazine, 7, 20-24.

Jones, M. G., Jones, B.D, Hardin, B., Chapman, L., Yarbrouth, T. & Davis, M. (1999). The impact of high-stakes testing on teacher and students in North Carolina. Phi Delta Kappan, 81, 199-203.

McLeskey, J., & Waldron, N. L. (1995). Inclusive elementary programs: Must they cure students with learning disabilities to be effective? Phi Delta Kappan, 77, 30-303.

Meier, D. (1998). Can the odds be changed? Phi Delta Kappan, 79, 358-362.

Messick, S., & Popham, W. J. (1997). What's wrong and what's right with rubrics. Educational Leadership, 72-75.

Morgan, D. (1998). Administering a middle school budget efficiently. Schools in the Middle, 7, 18-20.

Rinne, C. H. (1998). Motivating students is a percentage game. Phi Delta Kappan, 79, 620-628.

Roberts, J. L. (1999). The top 10 events creating gifted education for the new century. <u>Gifted Child Today Magazine, 22,</u> 53-55.

Rozycki, E. G. (1997). Cutting public school costs intelligently: Can it be done? <u>Educational Horizons, 76,</u> 8-10.

Smith, A.E., Morrow, J.E., & Gray, D.L. (1999). Principals educate beginning teachers about the law. <u>Education (Chula Vists, California)</u>, 120, 60-63.

Smith, M. K. (1999). Parents and teachers need to know. <u>Journal of Staff Development, 20, 72.</u>

Trujillo, P. A. (1998). Safe and legal. <u>Thrust for Educational Leadership, 6,</u> 20-24.

Walker, H. M.,& Gresham, F. M. (1997). Making schools safer and violence free. <u>Intervention in School and Clinic, 32,</u> 199-204.

Winicki, B. (1995). Full inclusion for students with disabilities. <u>Administrator's Notebook, 36,</u> 1-6.

Wober, C. L. (1999). Celebrating our future by revisiting our past. <u>Gifted Child Today Magazine, 22,</u> 58-61.

Zirkle, C. J. (1999). A primer on teacher liability. <u>Tech Directions, 59,</u> 32-34.

CHAPTER 12

The Adolescent's Perception of Failure

William Kritsonis, Ph.D.
McNeese State University
Lake Charles, LA

Upwards of a thousand students commit suicide every year. They had their whole lives ahead of them, but somehow, they lost hope. No one cared, they thought; life was not worth living. They asked themselves: "Is that all there is?" Suicide is certainly the ultimate self-punishment for having failed. Life is no longer worth the struggle or the effort.

I would like to take a look with you at the concept of failure: at how adolescents in high school and college see it; and what we, as parents and teachers, have taught them about it. The world is full of people who are fearful that they will fail at some task or goal and who usually manage to avoid trying because they construe failure as the worst of all possible crimes. We have all had a part in failure, all had to come to grips with it, and all had to decide what failure actually means to each of us individually.

Success is important in our society, more important, surely, than the desire to live sanely and to enjoy the good things of life,

257

which one has worked for. Success for its own sake is valued--valued, I believe, at any cost, and the road to success rationalized in the name of the great American competitive way, at the expense of honesty, and perhaps sanity.

The "F" for failure has become so feared that we in education have revamped our marking system in preference for U's and E's without revamping our attitudes-attitudes of those who should know.

We are apt to be very objective when we look at our students. We give them what they desire, and in doing so, we feel very smug. We have given out the material, we have given the examinations, and now it follows, as night follows day, we give out the marks. Yet we forget that there is much more that a teacher gives to his students, willingly or unwillingly. A teacher gives an example of how to look at life and at people. And if failure is viewed as the worst fate, if it is something that is given the connotation of shame, unworthiness, and hopelessness, then indeed, we have taught much more than English or history or mathematics.

Adolescence marks the trying period of search, which may have the significant effects on subsequent personality structure, and on later adjustments in the years that lie ahead. Probably, what brings the greatest amount of equalizing balance to the period of adolescence is the presence of significant people in the adolescent's life. Since people become so very important to an adolescent, it is the importance of those people who possess that special ingredient of compassion, who can help the adolescent come through this unfolding, transitional period into the fullness of adult life.

It is important to realize that in most competitive situations, two major motives appear: either to achieve success... or to avoid failure. The strivers-for-success are more likely to be middle-of-the-roaders in their aspirations or ambitions, whereas the failure-avoider will be either excessively cautious or extravagantly reckless in the things he tries. Because failure is painful, a failure-avoider will choose either extreme rather than take the 50-50 chance.

A person's self-picture does reflect the evaluation of himself by the crucial figures of his interpersonal environment. Self-evaluation may be influenced by peers as much as by parents. Feelings of adequacy and success may depend more on self-acceptance than on actual achievement. Regardless of actual test performance, self-accepting students tend to be optimistic, non-anxious, and non-competitive. Self-rejecting ones are anxious and unrealistic in goal setting.

A study was done where the subjects were asked to rate themselves on a list of traits as they *thought* they were, as they *hoped* they were, as they feared they were, and as they *thought* others regarded them. The groups had first been classified as stable and unstable on the basis of personality inventory. The stable group rated themselves higher showing less discrepancy between their self-ratings and the way they thought others would rate them. They were also better liked, better adjusted socially, less situation dominated, and showed less defensive behavior.

Approximately half of the students who enter college drop out. Many are in the highest levels of ability. When students drop out, it usually is understood that they have failed. At the college level, a great deal of attention has been given to the question: "What can we learn about those who have failed in the past that will enable us to reject similar persons who might apply for admission in the future?" Little consideration is given to the question: "What might the institution do to prevent failure, to help remedy shortcomings within the college and with the individual student, which produces failure?"

Reasons for coming to college are always multiple. Stress is usually placed on one or another or these:

- desire of getting a high paying job

- status of a degree
- social life--all my friends are going
- avoid joining work force
- get married
- pressure from parents

Many are disillusioned with what is expected of them. Many find that college is the same old things as high school--all these things which *are not practical.* Others who are eager to learn find that college is not the kind of challenge they had expected.

Many students entering college regret the time they wasted in high school. They did not try hard enough; they did not apply themselves; they were more interested in athletics, social life, or other things. Reflecting back, one may find many things that a student was concerned about during high school days--some things indeed far more important to the student than geometry or American history. Some interests were *far more necessary* and pressing in order that the student might mature. But, those who observed the adolescent in high school are very often unaware of what he is facing and are not able to understand why he can't buckle down. What one may not understand is the reason that there are many things the adolescent is trying to accomplish and school work often provides him with no stimulation, no incentive for interest or involvement. School is just a bore! And teachers are a bore! And adults, in general, are a bore! Adults are forever talking, but what they say often does not seem to *mean* anything.

A new interest can be sparked in school when there is a teacher who does mean something. But it takes more than one teacher to make a school program relevant. When competition and success are the significant ingredients of a program and when we are apt to be creating egocentric intellectuals who gloat over their achievements while looking down on those who have developed feelings of worthlessness and fear that they will probably never win, we are confirming that only those who win are important.

Our task ought to be providing help to the adolescent to see that failure is neither good nor bad. It is, however, an inevitable fact of reality that the way we use failure in our lives will determine, ultimately, its goodness or badness for *us*.

Each of us must learn to live with certain limitations in ability. It is only when an individual falls consistently below the norm in areas that *seem* important to him that inferior ability constitutes a serious limitation.

From studies of both high achievers and underachievers in high school, the pattern of the relationship between self-concept and achievement becomes clearer. A relationship is present between positive self-concept and high achievement, negative self-concept and underachievement, but research does not indicate which is cause or effect. Chances are we can see a circular pattern beginning earlier with perception or experiences. Every experience contributes to the adolescent's evolving picture of himself, which, in turn, becomes a guide to future action.

Parental pressure for success seems to arise naturally out of parents' desire that their children receive the best the world has to offer, yet in the same breath, it may be that many parents see the failure which their son or daughter may face as a failure for themselves. Many parents want their children to be a credit to them, forgetting that if a child is a credit to self, the other will follow naturally.

Likewise, importance should not be given to doing better than the next guy, but rather to trying to do our best. We should be our own chief and best competition. We cannot always achieve our goal, but we ought to find satisfaction in knowing we did the best we could. Too often, we are teaching the idea of striving for success in high school, in college, in athletics, in all the aspects of living for the *wrong* reasons. Let's change our own attitudes about success and failure.

CHAPTER 13

Urban Schools: Challenges for the New Millennium

Linda L. Lebert, Ph. D.,
Assistant Professor-
Director of Curriculum Materials Center
McNeese State University
Lake Charles, LA

American education today is continually being studied through giant microscopic eyes that often reveal a myriad of problems and concerns. With increased media coverage, increased educational research, and numerous educational consultants, no educational entity goes without constant public, private, and government scrutiny. Evaluation and challenges to improve should not be viewed as being necessarily negative. Oftentimes, the evaluation does look at school systems with suggested designs that focus on school improvement or school empowerment. The important question to ask remains the same: How will suggested designs improve the educational environment for the students?

One area of the educational environment that has been evaluated and re-evaluated is the entity of urban schools. Farber and Ascher tell us that urban schools have experienced troubles and endured many waves of reform. Many of the reforms, however, often seem far removed from daily school activities and thus leave teachers with increased feelings of burnout (Farber & Ascher, 2000). When focusing on urban schools, one must remember that this type of school is usually a "vast web of interconnected social problems" (Burnett, 1996). All too often, the suggested new designs or reforms for urban schools address areas other than the many social problems that hamper effective learning. Teachers desire and strive to make a difference in the lives of their students. They need to know of immediate support toward improving student life and student learning.

An added dimension of the urban schools is the poverty that exists for urban children. Life for urban parents is an increasing economic battle in which we find single females raising children on very low wages or under the added strain of unemployment (Ascher, 1988). One would be remiss to overlook the significance of the level of poverty that exists among the student population in urban schools. We live in a society that is comfortable in the sense of material goods, food, clothing, and shelter. When basic needs such as these are not met, there results a student population that attends school lacking proper nutrition, adequate clothing, and, oftentimes, stressed about the poverty that exists in the home

266

environment. Effective learning will be hampered if these aspects are overlooked.

Other detrimental influences on urban schools are the problems associated with the financing of these schools. School budgets play a paramount role in all schools. State education budgets have not kept up with inflation. The states have not had the money to replace federal dollars that may have been deleted. State aid to school districts actually discriminates against urban schools because funding is based on the Average Daily Attendance. Urban school districts have high absentee rates. An added burden is the fact that state support does not keep up with increasing expenses (Ascher, 1989).

Finally, the focus of reform in America tends to spotlight "excellence rather than equality." Therefore, extra state dollars are being distributed to excellence projects and bypassing the disadvantaged urban students (Ascher, 1989). Excellence in and of itself is a wonderful goal to strive toward, but simple needs regarding student concerns must be addressed initially. By doing this, programs of excellence will be established in situations where success will be attainable.

Some previous reforms that have tried to address the needs of urban schools have included "partnerships, collaborative program delivery, strategic planning, and new governance structures" (Rural and Urban School Finance, 1995). At present, much research has been done on the successes and failures of such reforms. The question at hand is "What about now?" Where does one look for hope in urban schools in this new millennium? Where can the answers be found that will address the concerns of urban students, empower teachers in urban schools, and facilitate overall reform in urban schools?

What about today's focus on technology? Is America's focus on technology-proficient education and the general goal of preparing students in a technology-rich working world going to play a major part in the current efforts at reform in all schools as well as urban schools? How are the added challenges of technology affecting urban schools in America?

Technology and the many related terms associated with technology have become the current "buzz words" among educational experts. Technology is being implemented to improve the educational system throughout the United States, a system that is lacking in a number of ways. All too often, people look for answers or try to find a panacea for problems and want it implemented immediately into nearby school systems. Burnett tells us that technology transformation in the United States is not as rapid as some may think. Some students obtain only minimal training in computers without any clear purpose for utilization. There is also a very wide range of possibilities when one is dealing with educational technology. Programs that provide games, word-processing, graphics, multimedia systems, and the Internet are but a few of the tools that are available for use in educational systems (Burnett, 1994).

If technology is to provide a prominent place in urban schools, educators must "clarify the role of computers as a pedagogical tool, define its relationship to existing curricula, and establish the level of human and financial investment" (Burnett, 1994). Once schools clarify the role of technology and establish a relationship to curricula, the avenues for technology delivery become unlimited. The major limitations are the vision (or lack thereof) of the administrators, and the funding to support the purchase and continued growth of technology. Burrus states that education, business and government need to unify and become "excited and involved in building a better tomorrow by discovering creative applications of technology tools." He states that to ensure effective integration of relevant technology into education, we must decide where we want to be in ten years. The vision that is projected must allow for growth in accomplishing projected success. Burrus also believes that technology that is currently in our schools is being under-utilized. Enhancement of the current learning experiences with the use of technology is an important factor (Norman, 2000).

There are incredible opportunities that could be provided with the utilization of distance learning in urban schools. Distance learning provides opportunities to reach larger audiences, to provide services for those who cannot physically attend classes at a college campus, to link students with other students of varying backgrounds, and to provide speakers from outside an educational system (Barry, 1992). It is of interest to note that almost all major universities are working on an experimental basis with offering courses on the Internet. Many are providing degrees and certificates through distance learning (Charp, 1998).

Distance learning is one method of service delivery that could provide urban school districts with high-quality educational opportunities. The concept of distance learning began in the nineteenth century. Modified ideas such as videotapes, broadcasts, satellites, and cable production came into being in the 1970's and 1980's. The delivery modes used today are linked with audio, video, and computer video conferencing technologies (Majdalany & Guiney, 1999).

Three elements to consider in the development of effective distance learning programs include:

*sound instructional design

*appropriate technology applications

*support for teachers, students, and collaborative partners.

Once these elements are dealt with, distance learning programs could be implemented with a number of benefits. Students could participate in honors and enrichment classes even though enrollment would be low. Links to outstanding enrichment programs could be established to include such entities as the Lincoln Center in New York City. Linking with remote guest speakers, businesses, and community colleges could enhance learning. College level courses, alternate education, and special education courses could be offered to urban students (Majdalany & Guiney, 1999).

Two programs that have incorporated excellent teaching strategies with technology include: the TEAMS project in Los Angeles, CA and The Learning Cafe. The TEAMS project allows students, teachers, and parents in more than ten states accessibility to programs that include workplace skills, life skills, higher mathematics and hands-on science activities. A variety of learners are served through this instructional programming to include K-12

271

students, adult learners, disabled students and limited-English-proficient students. All programming is provided through satellite, television, multimedia, and the Internet. The Learning Cafe is a program in Brooklyn, New York that has four 30-seat computer laboratories connected to the Internet. Web-based pre-college and college level courses are offered to urban students who are not likely to attend universities. Career options or college careers can be evaluated. Those students who chose to complete early college core courses (at no cost) are admitted to Brooklyn College (Majdalany & Guiney, 1999).

Programs such as the two mentioned show but a tip of the iceberg. There are vast possibilities in utilizing technology that are limited in development only by the lack of initiative or imagination in planning. Once a idea is developed, funding must be obtained. Grants, funding for at-risk programs, endowments, and special site-based funding are but a few of the creative methods that can be used to assure that innovative programs can be supported in urban schools. The entire "public relations" focus must be centered on the students and their needs and potential growth. There is no obstacle when using student focus in selling a new program to school boards, administration, or parents. A final key is enthusiasm! Enthusiasm coupled with thorough planning and funding can make or break a program. Enthusiasm is a tool that can become infectious to all involved in a new program. The final message is one of hopeful vision into a future in which educators can look at urban schools with "eyes wide open" and explore and implement technology-based programs that will expand and enhance the educational environment of urban school students.

References

Ascher, C. (1988, Mar). Improving the school-home connection for low-income urban parents. ERIC Clearinghouse on Urban Education (ED293973). Online. http://www.ed.gov/databases/ERIC-Digests/ed293973.html (2000, April 11).

Ascher, C. (1989). Urban school finance: the quest for equal educational opportunity. ERIC Clearinghouse on Urban Education (ED 311147) Online. http://www.ed.gov/databases/ERIC_Digests/ed311147.html (2000, April 11).

Barry, W. (1992, Nov.) Strategies for teaching at a distance. ERIC Digest (ED351008). Online. http://www.ed.gov/databases/ERIC_Digests/ed351008.html (2000, April 1).

Burnett, G. (1994, Feb). Technology as a tool for urban classrooms. ERIC Clearinghouse on Urban Education (ED368 809) Online. http://www.ed.gov/databases/ERIC_Digests/ed368809.html. (2000, April 11).

Burnett, G. (1996). Urban teachers and collaborative school-linked services. ERIC Clearinghouse on Urban Education Digest 96. Online. http://eric-web.tc.columbia.edu/digests/dig96.html. (2000, April 4).

Charp, S. (1998, Nov). Distance learning. T.H.E. Journal, 26, 4.

Farber, B. & Ascher, C. (2000). Urban school restructuring and teacher burnout. ERIC Clearinghouse on Urban Education Digest 75. Online. http://eric-web.tc.columbia.edu/digests/dig75.html. (2000, April 4).

Majdalany, G. & Guiney, S. (1999, Dec.). Implementing distance leaning in urban schools. ERIC Clearinghouse on Urban Education Digest 150. Online. http://eric-web.tc.columbia.edu/digests/dig150.html. (2000, April 4).

Norman, M. (2000, April). Daniel Burrus: Education, technology and the future. Converge, 60-62.

Rural and Urban School Finance: Districts and Experts Speak Out. Policy Briefs. Report 1, 1995. ED384121 Online. (2000, April 11).

MELLEN STUDIES IN EDUCATION